D1432948

The Grover E. Murray Studies in the American Southwest

In the Shadow of the Carmens

In the Shadow of the Carmens

Afield with a Naturalist in the Northern Mexican Mountains

Bonnie Reynolds McKinney

Foreword by David H. Riskind

Texas Tech University Press

This book is typeset in Monotype Amasis. The paper used in this book meets the minimum requirements of ANSI/NISO Z39.48–1992 (R1997). ∞

Designed by Kasey McBeath
Jacket photos by Bonnie Reynolds McKinney

Library of Congress Cataloging-in-Publication Data
McKinney, Bonnie Reynolds.
    In the shadow of the Carmens : afield with a naturalist in the northern Mexican mountains / Bonnie Reynolds McKinney ; foreword by David H. Riskind.
        p. cm. — (The Grover E. Murray studies in the American Southwest)
    Summary: "A naturalist's chronicle of the Carmen Mountains of northern Mexico; essays and photographs reflect the region's biodiversity, natural history, resources, and conservation"— Provided by publisher.
    Includes bibliographical references and index.
    ISBN 978-0-89672-764-9 (hardcover : alk. paper) — ISBN 978-0-89672-765-6 (e-book) 1. Natural history—Mexico, North. 2. Biodiversity—Mexico, North. 3. Nature conservation—Mexico, North. I. Title.
    QH107.M35 2012
    508.972—dc23   2012021872

Printed in the United States of America
12 13 14 15 16 17 18 19 20 / 9 8 7 6 5 4 3 2 1

Texas Tech University Press
Box 41037 | Lubbock, Texas 79409–1037 USA
800.832.4042 | ttup@ttu.edu | www.ttupress.org

This book is dedicated to "the Carmens"—may they remain forever wild under Coahuila blue skies.

Bonnie Reynolds McKinney

Coahuila, Mexico
2012

Contents

Illustrations

Photographs

Places of Interest in the Carmen Mountains

Map by J. D. Villalobos

1. Los Pilares headquarters
2. Santa Salomé
3. Los Frijoles
4. La Noria de Boquillas
5. Military checkpoint, Boquillas
6. Boquillas del Carmen
7. Cañón del Diablo
8. Rancho Los Ureste
9. Campo Dos
10. La Mesa Bonita
11. Campo Tres
12. La Mesa Escondido
13. Campo Cinco
14. Cuadra Pelota
15. La Cachuchua
16. Los Cojos
17. Cañón el Álamo
18. Cañón Morteros
19. La Linda, Coahuila
20. Rancho Casa Blanca
21. El Veinte
22. Pico Etero
23. Pila de Agua Chile
24. El Jardín
25. El Cerro del Alasan
26. Pico Centinela
27. Hacienda Piedra Blanca
28. Ejido Morelos
29. Cañón Botella
30. El Club
31. Campo Uno
32. La Laguna
33. Cañón Carboneras
34. Puerta Lince
35. Cañón Temblores
36. Rancho Guadalupe
37. Cañón Fronteriza and Fronteriza Mines
38. Chamiceras
39. Casa San Isidro
40. Cañón Juárez
41. Cañón Moreno
42. Hacienda Santo Domingo
43. Mesa de los Fresnos
44. Pico Loomis
45. Cuesta Malena
46. El Melón
47. Cerro Ombligo
48. Puerta Poblano
49. Cerro El Conejo
50. Los Pilares
51. La Caldera
52. Cañón el Oso
53. Rio Bravo del Norte (Rio Grande)

All the naturalists I've known working in the greater Big Bend National Park have been drawn to the sheer limestone cliffs of the Sierra del Carmen, and particularly the highest peak, Pico Cerdo (known as the Schott Tower in far-west Texas), located across the Rio Grande in Coahuila, Mexico. To the south and east is the jagged Sierra del Jardín—with Pico Centinela as its highest point—and the contiguous Maderas del Carmen whose high mesas and canyons shelter a magnificent mixed conifer forest. First called the El Carmen by the U.S.–Mexico Boundary Survey, the toponym probably referred only to the limestone range cut by the Rio Grande. The mountain massif remains a significant corridor for biota along the Madrean–Rocky Mountain axis. This combined range straddles the divide between the Chihuahuan Desert to the west and the Tamaulipan Province to the east. The grand Chisos Mountains are in the rain shadow cast by Carmen topography. One of the great pleasures of experiencing the Carmens is to sit in the saddle below and just to the north of the highest peak, Loomis, and watch Gulf weather do battle, and lose, with the resulting basin and range aridity. Every surviving drop of precipitation makes its way to the Rio Grande and thence to the Gulf of Mexico.

In the 1930s, Ernest G. Marsh, Jr., a student working in the Chisos Mountains, was the first to study the flora and fauna of this terrain, and he had intended to use the research for a dissertation at the University of Texas in Austin. Although this work was never completed nor published, as World War II intervened, he did submit a report to the National Park Service in 1936, titled "Biological Survey of the Santa Rosa and del Carmen Mountains of Northern Coahuila, Mexico."

C. H. Muller studied the plants of the area as part of his investigation of the vegetation of Coahuila, Mexico. Many of Muller's collections centered in the area of El Club and Cañón Centinela at the northern end of the igneous ranges. He never met Marsh, but C. H. told me that in the mid-1930s he saw some tire tracks heading south toward Múzquiz near Piedra Blanca and these surely must have belonged to Ernest.

Investigators such as W. B. Taylor led expeditions to the Carmens in 1945 to document the wildlife and assess the potential of the area as an element of an International Peace Park. His team reported their findings in 1946 as "The Sierra del Carmen in northern Coahuila, a preliminary ecological survey." A few collections were made by Frederic W. Miller, associated with the Dallas Museum of Natural History, who visited the mountains with a hunting party and who was honored (in 1947 by H. Jackson) with his name becoming the specific epithet for a rare Carmen Mountain shrew, now known as Miller's shrew (*Sorex milleri*).

Rollin H. Baker and a cadre of students worked the area, especially the lower and mid-elevations, in the early 1950s. Baker summarized this work on area mammals in the classic *Mammals of Coahuila*, published in 1956. At about the same time, Alden H. Miller conducted extensive investigations on the area's birdlife, published in 1955 as "The Avifauna of the Sierra del Carmen of Coahuila, Mexico."

My colleague Ro Wauer has observed and reported on the Carmen's birds since the late 1960s and, more recently, on Lepidoptera; my botanist colleagues and I have documented the area's flora extensively for nearly four decades.

Importantly, this fraternity of "ologists" has investigated the greater Carmen ecosystem in some detail over the years and, on occasion, stayed in the field for several weeks. But no one has *lived* in the Carmens, carefully observing and taking in the landscape, wildlife, weather, and sunrises and sunsets on a daily basis, year after year, for over a decade. Bonnie has!

Her keen eye, along with her skills as an observer and investigator, has paid off richly. Her artistic skills and verbal talent have painted a rich and diverse landscape of the Carmens and of its inhabitants and moods—from glorious sunny days through months of drought, to snow and ice storms and endless days of impenetrable, chilling fog, to unrelenting sleet, hail, or tropics-inspired deluge.

Bonnie has infected the El Carmen Project staff with the mission to plug burning biological gaps with amazing results, such as recording the capture and documentation of the Coahuila mole (*el topo de Coahuila*) at El Club at long last. Rollin Baker was made proud! Bonnie also collaborated with Jonás A. Delgadillo Villalobos, Feliciano H. Pineda, and Santiago G. Isern in documenting the nest of the tiny, secretive Miller's shrew. Again Rollin beamed.

And, on a grander scale, Bonnie has studied the Maderas' black bear population and proved how common they are in the mountains. Through her tireless telemetric studies, we now know about their home ranges, health, and reproductive success in that rugged terrain. I am not even going to try and summarize her multiple contributions to bighorn sheep and elk restoration projects.

Her tireless work with cooperating biologists and her enthusiasm that has inspired many students are legacies that will continue well beyond her tenure in the Carmens. We are hopeful that she will continue her work for many more years in one of the most diverse and ecologically intact of the world's sky islands.

In the meantime, enjoy the images she paints with words. You will also hear the sounds of black bears foraging, the call of the common black hawk, and perhaps, just perhaps, the faint call of *el lobo*.

Bravo to Bonnie Reynolds McKinney, Wildlife Coordinator, CEMEX-Proyecto El Carmen, Maderas del Carmen, Coahuila, Mexico.

David H. Riskind
Austin, Texas
2012

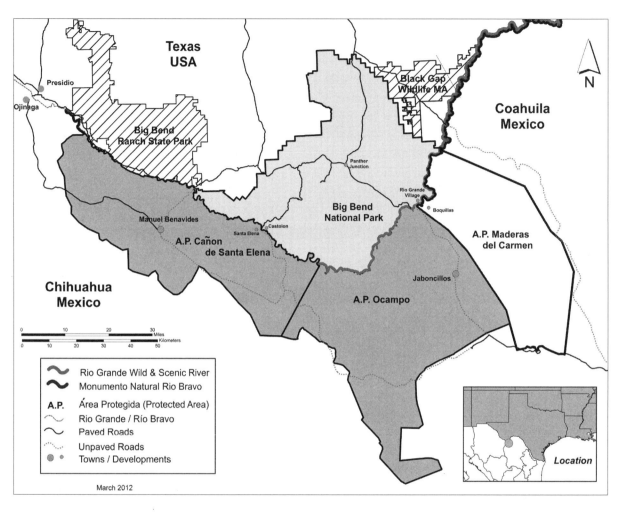

The Texas-Mexico borderlands. Map by Betty Alex, produced by Big Bend National Park, Texas.

Acknowledgments

I am grateful to CEMEX for giving me the opportunity to live and work in the Carmens. I also thank my husband Billy Pat and my son Matt and daughter-in-law Julia for their support. I wish to thank the staff at El Carmen for their support and assistance—everyone who works at El Carmen contributes in many ways to the success of this large conservation project. I also extend my appreciation to Billy Pat McKinney, Santiago Gibert Isern, and Jim Brock for the use of their photographs in this book. Many thanks to Jonás Delgadillo Villalobos for the use of many of his photos and for the design of the Carmen Mountains place names map. Thanks also to Betty Alex at Big Bend National Park for her rendering of the borderlands map. I greatly appreciate the reading and critique of this manuscript by David Riskind and Andrew Sansom—their insights were quite valuable. I am honored to have David Riskind write the foreword for my book, as he knows and appreciates the Carmen Mountains, having spent much time there. I thank the many people who have helped me during my career working with wildlife over the years, and particularly Mike Pittman and Dr. Clyde Jones. I also thank Texas Tech University Press for publishing my book—Judith Keeling and Joanna Conrad deserve special thanks for all their help and answering my many questions. Without their help this book would not have been possible.

Lastly, but most importantly, I thank my parents, the late Garvis M. Reynolds and Katie Reynolds. They were always there, and dealt with my many escapades while I was growing up. My dad once asked my mom, "How does Bonnie find the places she lives in?" Daddy, you would have loved the Carmens.

In the Shadow of
the Carmens

1   # The Carmens

For twenty-two years I lived on the Texas-Mexico border, and every day that I was in the field conducting wildlife work, I never failed to look south to the great mountains in northern Coahuila. Those mountains were so fascinating to me that I could only imagine what natural treasures and untold secrets were hidden in their deep canyons and high peaks. I watched as the sun's dying rays turned the jagged peaks to fiery red and the canyons below to purple hues that artists will never capture on canvas. I watched as wildfires raged in the highlands, and as clouds covered the peaks, transforming the entire sierra into a dark mass that seemed to lie in wait, for what I didn't know. I saw dawn creep slowly forward, turning the gray shadowed mountain into hues of gold and pink, ready for another day, another century. For years I worked on various wildlife projects in Mexico, but never in the Carmens. Like a moth to flame I was drawn to those mountains, always close, but never on site. I flew over the Carmens countless times searching for peregrine falcon eyries and collecting radio telemetry on black bears and desert bighorns. I collected historical information earlier scientists had published, and I listened to borderland stories of cool forests, hot dry deserts, bears, pumas, and stories of lost gold and riches. I heard the mountains called the Fronterizas, Carmens, El Jardín, Maderas del Carmen, and Sierra del Carmen. Which mountain ranges were they? Now that I live and work within them, they have become one as they share the same ecological landscape, and they will always be "the Carmens."

I have lived in the Carmens for over ten years, and they have never disappointed me—they are all I imagined and more. Now that I am here, those nameless canyons, peaks, high mesas, and basins all have names and special meanings. "Chamiceras"—a tall waterfall, knee-deep grass, summer heat, and bats in old mines; "Mesa Bonita"—so quiet you only hear yourself breathing, high mountain meadows, and bear scratches on trees; "Cañón Juárez"—a fossil shell, a solitary eagle soaring over the canyon rim, and rain, snow, sleet, wind, and sun, all in twenty minutes' time; "Los Pilares"—counting bighorn lambs, inky dark desert night with great horned owls calling and car lights far away in the Big Bend of Texas; "Cañón Botella"—a jumbled boulder pile with a clear mountain stream, Mexican long-nosed bats, and golden eagles; "Mesa de los Fresnos"—a high grassland mesa, cactus blooms, and historic Mexican lobo habitat; "Campo Dos"—a stormy day in November, howling winds bending stately fir trees, clouds swirling on the ground, and time standing still. These are just a few of the special places. The mountain has many secret places: some should be shared, and some are kept in my memory so that I can go to that special place in my mind when I need to. The Carmens are many things: the people, the flora and fauna, the culture, the history, and the land itself. All are important in this diverse ecosystem.

The Carmens are fragile desert where a diminutive black-tailed gnatcatcher feeds her young in a tiny, woven cup-shaped nest hidden in a creosote bush. They are the sheer arrogance of a peregrine falcon screaming as he rides the wind along the high escarpment, diving like the proverbial silver bullet at the red-tailed hawk that dares invade his territory. High on the limestone escarpment in a depression of pink and gray limestone, his mate silently watches all, her warm feathers incubating two dark, blotched eggs under her body. Higher on the forested slopes and in cool, moist canyons, a Carmen Mountain white-tailed deer stamps his foot at annoying insects while he feeds on succulent meadow grasses. Ambling slowly along, a black bear takes her three cubs to a clear stream of trickling water. The cubs splash and play in the creek while she rests under a towering Coahuila fir tree.

Miles down the mountain, through the sotol-yucca foothills and out across the desert flats to a jumble of rocks forming a small desert island, a magnificent desert bighorn ram, his head crowned with massive curled horns, stands surveying his domain from the highest peak. Below him on the slopes, ewes and lambs feed on rich chino grama grass. The ram is so still he appears carved from stone. Slowly turning his head at a noise, he sees nothing threatening or otherwise, but his very sensitive ears have alerted him to a presence. A large, tawny puma lies flattened behind a rock;

not even his whiskers move, his golden eyes pinned on the bighorn, as he waits patiently. He is tired, having come from the north in Texas last night on silent feet, padding across the desert to reach these mountains. High in a mountain canyon, a waterfall plunges through jumbled rocks to a foaming pool below; a bull elk lifts his muzzle from the cool water and bugles his challenge to all who will listen.

But the Carmens were not always this way. They have persisted, perhaps sometimes teetering on the brink; they have lost species and accepted new ones. The Carmens have seen it all. Surely this sierra is a "she," for she nurtures the land, the people, the plants, and animals from the tiniest wildflower to the biggest black bear. She has felt the pain of losing her forest to loggers, thousands of trees cut and left lying where they fell. But she didn't give up; instead she created a wind to dislodge the seeds, wildfires to sear the hard seed pods, a gentle rain to soak them, and warm sun to germinate the seeds in the nutritious soil to sprout new trees. She has seen death and life, each is a give-and-take. An old bear enters his den to hibernate for the last time; he is weary, he sleeps and never wakes, his bones will eventually turn to dust. Just down the canyon a mother bear gives birth to two tiny cubs. After hearing the last lobo howl, the sierra thought, no more, they are gone. She has endured pounding rains flooding canyons, droughts so extreme the prickly pear turned yellow, bone-chilling cold when ice cov-ered everything and tree limbs snapped like matchsticks, and winter snows that transformed her into a fairyland, so silent and white, not even a bird singing. She shifted and adjusted. This sierra must have grown very jaded at times, but she continues in her never-ending struggle to keep the balances right so that all may coexist. She has been battered, bruised, and scarred, but now at last human activities are guided by a gentler spirit than in times past. This mountain has endured for eons, and another rebirth is under way, where once again desert bighorn rams will square off and clash horns, fighting over ewes, elk will bugle in the mountains, bear cubs will play in mountain meadows, desert mule deer will polish their antlers on sotol plants, and perhaps, just perhaps, one day in the future the Mexican lobo will once again lift his silver muzzle to the sky and howl his plaintive song. How is this happening?

The Carmens have been famous for many years, as far back as 1747 when the governor of Coahuila, Pedro de Rábago, led an expedition to these mountains (Luis Elizondo, pers. comm., 2005). Later, Comanches and Apaches came out of the north on horses, splashing across the Rio Bravo del Norte, and they raided ranches and stole horses, cattle, and women. Smugglers carved paths through the inhospitable mountains crossing into Texas with illegal liquor made from sotol plants. Cattlemen brought in livestock by the droves. This land was rich, the grass would never give out, wildlife was plentiful, and water was abundant. Goats, cattle, and horses by the thousands grazed in a pattern that would last well over two hundred years. Subsoil riches were discovered, and mining for lead, silver, and fluorspar began, and thousands of miners moved into the area. Riparian galley forests of cottonwood trees were cut for mine supports, cattle trampled the new seedlings, and the regeneration process for the cottonwood came to an abrupt halt. Miners needed food and lots of it. Commercial hunters were hired and the native game rapidly declined. The mule deer, Carmen Mountain white-tail, black bear, javelina, desert bighorn, pronghorn, and smaller game all fell victim to the commercial hunters, and subsistence hunting on a year-round basis continued by local residents. Ranchers on the northern side of the river brought steel traps and poison to help in the eradication of the Mexican lobo, which was thought to be a true menace to all who had livestock. In the process of trapping and poisoning lobos, many black bears as well as other species became victims of the traps and poisons. Untold acres of grasslands were depleted, native wildlife numbers reached all-time lows, and three species of native wildlife were totally eradicated—the Mexican lobo, pronghorn, and desert bighorn. The desert bighorn was not only hunted but also contracted diseases from domesticated sheep and goats. Natural mortality, unregulated hunting, domesticated livestock diseases, and loss of habitat all took tremendous tolls on wildlife. The black bear hung

on in remnant populations in a few isolated mountain ranges, particularly the Carmens, Serranías del Burro, Sierra Encantada, and Sierra Santa Rosa, all in northern Coahuila, and in a few sierras in the adjacent state of Chihuahua.

In 1944, just across the Rio Bravo del Norte, the Big Bend National Park was created, and plans began for an international park that would include the Carmen Mountains in Mexico. However, lack of resources, inaccessibility, and World War II likely explain why the plans never became a reality. Today probably the most photographed scene in the Big Bend Park is not in the park, but across the Rio Bravo del Norte in Coahuila where the massive limestone face of the Sierra del Carmen rises from the desert floor, towering over the landscape, below where the tiny village of Boquillas del Carmen lies nestled against the base of the escarpment.

Scientists periodically visited the Carmens, describing new plant and animal species, and endemic species were discovered, but still the land continued to be heavily exploited. From the 1920s to the 1970s, the high forest was commercially logged: thousands of trees were cut, and many were left lying on the forest floor where they fell. Sawmills were constructed, more people moved to the mountain, and mining operations also continued. The candelilla plant, known for its wax by-product, was harvested by the ton in the lower desert elevations.

Yet people persisted in their dreaming and

scheming of ways to conserve this uniquely biodiverse ecosystem. Reminiscent of the southern Appalachian Mountains, American basswood and dogwood trees grow alongside Coahuila fir, prickly pear cactus, and maguey plants. Several small mammal species in northern Coahuila were discovered and scientifically documented, including the Coahuila mole, Miller's shrew, and cliff chipmunk. Many people knew of the unique biodiversity of this mountain chain, but financial resources were in short supply, access was limited, and most field trips were of short duration. In 1956, Dr. Rollin Baker conducted the most comprehensive fieldwork on the mammals of the area, and these observations provided the building blocks for future studies of the mammalian fauna.

In 1994, the Mexican government officially declared the greater Maderas del Carmen–Sierra del Carmen ecosystem the "Área de Protección de Flora y Fauna Maderas del Carmen." However, all lands remained in private hands or communal *ejidos* (for keeping livestock) and traditional land use continued. Several years later CEMEX commenced buying lands that were for sale in the Carmens. This was the beginning of the El Carmen Project, and a long-term commitment of resources and attention by CEMEX, with the ultimate goal of restoring lands and native wildlife to ensure that this unique area would remain for future generations.

The El Carmen Project currently encompasses over 200,000 hectares of land under direct CEMEX ownership or conservation agreement with area landowners. From a management and restoration point of view, a formal baseline inventory of the flora and fauna using scientific methods became necessary. To manage a very large area with a total ecosystem approach, all species are important, not just one or a few. All species are considered and their distribution and habitat preferences documented. In total ecosystem management, management techniques are designed so that restoring or enhancing one species or its habitat is not detrimental to another species.

The El Carmen Project is centered on the west side of the Carmens, 60 kilometers south of the Big Bend Region in West Texas and 165 kilometers northwest of Múzquiz, Coahuila. This enormous sky island rises from the Chihuahuan Desert floor and culminates in a high-mountain pine and fir forest over nine thousand feet in elevation. The Carmens are part of the northern end of the Sierra Madre Oriental, and a part of a biogeographic corridor linking Mexico to the Rocky Mountains in the southwestern United States. To clarify the different areas, the northern part—the massive limestone fault block that visitors to the Big Bend National Park see across the Rio Grande—is called the Sierra del Carmen. The portion behind the escarpment contains the area known as Cañón del Diablo. Southeast of Diablo are the jagged igneous peaks of the Sierra del

Jardín; moving east, the peaks connect with the area known as Pico Centinela and farther east the El Club area. Towering over all this, but still connected, are the massive west-facing cliffs, rockslides, canyons, mesas, and forest that dominate the landscape—this is the Maderas del Carmen. The south-facing slopes are drained through the Cañón el Álamo and Cañón Fronteriza. The southern tip of the Maderas del Carmen contains the high grassland mesa called the Mesa de los Fresnos, which was formed by lava flows—-thus the name, "the Carmens," which covers the entire area.

The description of the geology of the Carmens is best left to an expert. Limestone and igneous rock, incredible rock formations with slides, spires, and steppes, lava flows, rhyolite cliffs, and much more all form the mass of this mountain chain. Water, wind, and time have also played an important part in the topography of the Carmens, shaping the landscape over thousands of years.

The Carmens are characterized by five major vegetation associations: desert shrub, grasslands, chaparral, oak-pine forest, and fir forest. The lower desert elevations are replete with typical Chihuahuan desert shrub, such as creosote bush, mesquite, prickly pear, lechuguilla, and candelilla. The transition zone is dominated by beaked yucca, giant white dagger, sotol, bear grass (looks like grass, but in reality is part of the lily family), and native grasses. The canyons and higher elevations are dominated by oaks, junipers, and several species of pines. The highest elevations are dominated by Douglas fir and Coahuila fir. Elevations vary greatly, from the desert floor at 1,000 meters to more than 2,700 meters in the higher elevations providing a relief of over 1,200 meters.

The Carmens' high escarpments serve as a break against the moisture-laden Gulf Coast air masses that bring most rainfall to the area. Several days of rainfall in the Carmens are common even when the Big Bend just across the border is sunny and cloudless. The heaviest rainfall occurs in mid to late summer and early fall. Winter snows, ice storms, and sleet are not uncommon.

Goldman (1951) divided Mexico into seven major life zones below the Artic-Alpine belt. The Carmens contain species of flora and fauna from five of the seven life zones, including the arid upper tropical subzone, lower austral zone, upper austral zone, transition zone, and Canadian zone. Goldman also included the Carmens in the Chihuahua-Zacatecas biotic province, which he divided into three biotic districts. The third was designated the Sierra del Carmen biotic district, based on its high elevation and the isolation that he thought formed a minor distribution center extending across the border to include the Chisos Mountains in Texas. It is rare that a single mountain chain has its own biotic district; this serves to highlight the Carmens' nonpareil biodiversity.

In 2001, after twenty-two years of living and working in the Black Gap Wildlife Management Area, my husband Billy Pat and I resigned from long-term employment with the Texas Parks and Wildlife Department to begin a second career with the CEMEX El Carmen Project in Coahuila. We had visited the area on weekends and during vacations for the past year, assisting with planning and preliminary field and habitat work. We weren't moving far, just across the river, but yet it was Mexico. I had wanted to live in Mexico for a number of years, and both Billy Pat and I had visited many parts of the country over the previous ten years. I was where I wanted to be, and hoped to stay for a long time.

Our jobs were different, as Billy Pat was the project manager and I was wildlife coordinator. He basically had the task of running the entire project, while I was in charge of the biological staff and wildlife survey work, along with research and general wildlife management duties.

The first biological crew consisted of me, Jonás Delgadillo Villalobos, Feliciano Heredia Pineda, Guillermo Figuero, and Mario Aranda. Biologists come and go—most work for a period of time and then return to school to complete master's and doctorate degrees. Field biologists are somewhat of a dying breed and, in today's world of computer modeling, it is becoming difficult to find biologists and field technicians who

are willing to work outdoors in all types of terrain and weather observing a myriad of species as well as conducting specific research projects. At the time of this writing, the wildlife staff was comprised of Jonás, Hugo Sotelo, Ramiro Vasquez, Beto Martinez, and me. We have weathered many storms, and have wondered sometimes why we were freezing on a mountain in July at four o'clock in the morning, catching bats, finishing up presentations just as the plane landed with guests, and documenting new species for the Carmens, while thinking, "Nobody will believe this!" We have accomplished a tremendous amount of fieldwork, and there is much more to do.

When the El Carmen Project began, our first step was to compile historical records to provide a baseline on the species found in the area. For the first several years we worked an average of twenty-one days per month in the field on some phase of baseline research as well as conducting three major research and wildlife restoration projects on black bear, elk, and desert bighorns. Our results to date have provided a comprehensive overview of the flora and fauna of the Carmen Mountains, but by no means is the overview completed. We found what we expected to find, but our expectations have been greatly surpassed by the wide range of species diversity in both flora and fauna. Overlapping habitats, niches, and a variety of vegetation associations have provided information to continue to build on the historical foundation of species previously present and absent and of past and ongoing changes in the flora and fauna. Several species of flora and fauna are rare, common, or reach the limit of their northern range in the Carmens, such as the red-flowered agave, Miller's shrew, cliff chipmunk, Mexican racer, and the endemic Coahuila mole. Key species of mammals that were not documented previously include the eastern fox squirrel, Virginia opossum (black phase), and porcupine.

The bat fauna of the Carmens is very diverse: twenty species have been documented, including the Mexican long-nosed bat, eastern red bat, western yellow bat, ghost-faced bat, and several myotis species.

Large and medium sized mammals are well represented in the area. Common mammals include the black bear, puma, bobcat, coyote, gray fox, and ringtail. The coati is a rare species, and little is known about the ecology of this species in northern Mexico. The long-tailed weasel has also been documented as a resident species and is quite common from the lower elevations to over 8,000 feet in the pine-fir forest. Currently a total of 91 species of mammals have been documented. Three species that have been historically observed but not officially documented by a photograph or a specimen: the ocelot, jaguarondi, and jaguar.

The bird life in the Carmens is quite diverse because of geographical location, topography, the wide variety of habitats, abundant water sources and food availability, and the protection of habitats for nesting. A total of 299 species of birds have been documented, and we expect this list to surpass 300 species in time. Common desert birds include the cactus wren, black-throated sparrow, loggerhead shrike, greater roadrunner, northern mockingbird, northern cardinal, pyrrhuloxia, verdin, and ladder-backed woodpecker. Mid-elevation resident birds include the Mexican jay, black-crested titmouse, bushtit, gray vireo, rock wren, and Bewick's wren. The pine-oak woodlands and fir forests are home to the peregrine falcon, northern goshawk, Cooper's hawk, golden eagle, yellow-eyed junco, Mexican jay, white-breasted and pygmy nuthatches, Audubon's oriole, and acorn woodpecker. Spring brings a host of birds that breed, raise their young, and then migrate south in the fall. A few of these are the yellow-breasted chat, painted redstart, summer tanagers and hepatic and western tanagers, blue grosbeak, indigo buntings and painted and varied buntings, hooded and Scott's orioles, and western and Cassin's klingbirds. Three species of quail inhabit the Carmens: the Montezuma quail is found in the pine-oak woodlands down into the transition zone, the lower elevations support the scaled quail, and the northern bobwhite is found only on the east side of the Carmens at the southern end in grassland and edge habitat below the mesas. Dove species are numerous: band-tailed pigeon, mourning dove, white-winged dove, white-tipped dove, common ground dove, and Inca dove are all resident species. Rio Grande wild turkeys are found from the pine-oak woodlands to the lower elevations.

Common hummingbirds include the Lucifer, magnificent, blue-throated, black-chinned, and broad-tailed. Nine species of owls have been observed: the barn owl, great horned owl, eastern and western screech owls, flammulated owl, elf owl, northern pygmy owl, northern saw-whet owl, and burrowing owl. The rare solitary eagle is a summer resident in the higher elevations in the pine-fir association, and represents range expansion in this species. In 2004, slate-throated redstarts were documented nesting in the pine-oak woodlands (McCormack et al. 2005), the first nesting record for the species in Coahuila. The numerous earthen tanks, mountain streams, and seeps provide a veritable oasis for migrating birds in spring and fall, and wintering grounds for a wide variety of shorebirds and waterfowl. High in the pine-oak woodlands there is a natural *laguna* (loosely, marshland or shallow lake) that provides wintering grounds for ducks and resting areas for shore birds during migration. In 1969, my friend, the late Bob Burleson, told me that he saw the laguna literally covered with snow geese during a winter visit he made to the area. Fall and winter bring a large variety of sparrows to the lower elevations, where they spend the winter feeding on grass and weed seeds. Common species in winter are Chipping, clay-colored, Brewer's, Savannah,

Lincoln's, song, vesper, and white-crowned sparrows.

Reptile and amphibian fauna are well represented by the documentation of sixty-five species, including the rare Trans-Pecos copperhead, Mexican racer, and gray-banded kingsnake.

Habitat restoration is a major priority at El Carmen. One of the earliest steps taken was the removal of domestic livestock (cattle, horses, goats, and burros). All lands are being rested and native grasses, forbs, and shrubs are rapidly regenerating. More than two hundred miles of interior fences were removed to allow freedom of movement for all wildlife species. Existing earthen tanks were cleaned and native plant growth encouraged. Water sources for wildlife were developed by a series of pipelines to areas of good habitat that lacked water sources. Existing water troughs used formerly by livestock were made wildlife friendly with cement, rock, and wooden ramps so that all species could water safely.

Riparian restoration is also a priority. Once canyons with live water supported huge stands of native cottonwoods. The live creeks remain but only a few ancient cottonwoods still stand. Replanting native cottonwoods to restore the riparian galley forests will help prevent soil erosion and provide nesting sites for many species of birds, including the common black hawk, a summer resident.

Native wildlife restoration is an ongoing project. After many years of unregulated hunting by area residents, as well as earlier commercial hunting, many native wildlife populations were very low. Desert mule deer were practically non-existent; by supplementing this population, we are not only ensuring that the population will reach viable numbers and continue to expand into former habitat, but we are also increasing genetic diversity. Although Carmen Mountain white-tailed deer numbers were not as low, supplementing this sky island population with genetic diversity was considered necessary. These deer prefer the higher pine-oak woodlands and the mule deer prefer the lower desert and foothills. The ranges of both species overlap in the foothills. Javelina have increased rapidly since hunting pressure has been removed. Small and medium-sized mammal populations appear to be abundant and healthy.

In 2000–2001, CEMEX, in collaboration with Agrupación Sierra Madre and Unidos para la Conservación, launched a very intense desert bighorn sheep restoration program. The first step was the construction of a five-thousand hectare (roughly 11,000 acres) breeding facility located at Los Pilares in the lower desert elevation. Desert bighorns were captured in Sonora, Mexico and transported to Los Pilares. The breeding facility is located in typical bighorn habitat encircled by a predator-proof fence. Because of its large size, the desert bighorns quickly adapted, forming groups and exhibiting behavior of free-ranging bighorns. A total of forty-eight bighorns were placed in the facility in 2000–2001, and from this herd surplus numbers are now available for wild release into the Carmens.

Elk were historically documented in Mexico, as evidenced by bones and teeth found in caves near Cuatro Ciénegas, Coahuila (Gilmore 1947), and by ancient indigenous pictographs that clearly depict elk. In 2003 an introduction program for Rocky Mountain elk began with the initial release of forty-one animals. These numbers were supplemented with an additional nineteen elk in 2004 and twenty more in 2005. These elk were obtained from existing herds in the adjacent Serranías del Burro, from David Garza Lagüera's Rancho Rincón.

The black bear is a keystone, flagship, and umbrella species, and a definite indicator species of environmental well-being. By the 1940s and 1950s, black bear numbers in Mexico were very low and had disappeared from much of their historical range. A few remnant populations survived in isolated mountain areas in northern Coahuila and adjacent Chihuahua. It is through these remnant populations that the black bear is recovering and expanding into its former historic rangeland. The reestablishment of small populations in western Texas was linked to northern Coahuila black bear populations by mtDNA analysis of tissue and hair samples in genetic work conducted by Dave Onorato (Onorato 2001). With this expanding population, the need arose for information on all aspects of black bear ecology. Black bear research and conservation has been a major priority at El Carmen. Recently we completed a long-term project that began in 2003 involving various parameters of black bear ecology in the Carmen Mountains (McKinney and Delgadillo 2007). We also translated into Spanish a manual for handling black bears that I had written previously, and CEMEX published it in 2005. The *Manual para el manejo del oso negro mexicano* is free of charge to agencies, landowners, and interested persons who are currently handling black bears in Mexico.

Students working on their master's and doctorate degrees from Mexican and U.S. universities are conducting fieldwork in El Carmen and being supported by El Carmen in various ways. The El Carmen staff also conducts research as well as participating in local and international conferences and workshops. For several years, the El Carmen Project sponsored an international workshop. Mexican and Texas universities sent students and professors to El Carmen for a weeklong workshop on conducting baseline inventories of flora and fauna and selected wildlife management techniques taught by the El Carmen staff.

A number of local residents on nearby ejidos work full-time at El Carmen, many of whom had formerly hunted in the area and are now working daily to conserve and enhance wildlife and habitat. El Carmen works closely with area landowners, providing technical support in various wildlife programs, and several area ranchers are conservation partners. El Carmen is also involved locally and internationally with many conservation groups, including government agencies and non-governmental entities.

This is the Carmens: a land of contrasts and unequaled biodiversity; a sky island and the ultimate refuge. It is a land that has endured much hardship, but is now seeing a regeneration of lands, flora, and fauna. A fragile yet tough ecosystem that deserves the special attention it is now receiving through the generosity of CEMEX. The El Carmen Project can be a model for conservation and restoration efforts, not only locally but globally, to show what can be accomplished with time, commitment, and resources. El Carmen is not a park, but a vast ecosystem that has been set aside as a place for contiguous lands that have been restored to harbor the native flora and fauna that are an integral part of Mexico's rich biodiversity.

The essays in this book comprise an attempt to take you into the Carmens, acquainting you with some of its special places and natural resources, and with the efforts of CEMEX and the El Carmen team to restore the lands and wildlife and document the biodiversity of this great ecosystem. A lifetime would be necessary to document all the marvels that Mother Nature has bestowed upon this magnificent sierra just across the border from western Texas in the great state of Coahuila. It is my hope that you will gain awareness of and appreciation for this great sky island, a true jewel of biodiversity in a land where time stands still. I also hope you will appreciate the importance of the conservation work financed by a private corporation. This is truly a giant enterprise by CEMEX to restore and provide protection for an ecosystem that is the core of a large, contiguous land mass that supports ecological corridors connecting Mexico and the United States.

2 The Lobo Mexicano and Hacienda Santo Domingo

My first encounter with the Mexican lobo in Coahuila was in the form of a rug hanging on the wall at Hacienda Santo Domingo in April 1994. My longtime friend, rancher Chabela Spence Sellers, and I were spending the night at the Hacienda Santo Domingo, courtesy of owners Bobby and Bonnie Paul, so we could get an early start on a new breeding bird survey route we were establishing. The Santo Domingo is located on the eastern side of the Carmens, with the hacienda and ranch headquarters at the base of a large mesa. Looking east across a broad valley, the western side of the Serranías del Burro is breathtaking; grasslands give way to rough canyons and another mountain chain that is also replete with highly diverse flora and fauna.

After dinner, I took several photos of the lobo rug and noted that at least part of the original skull and teeth were in the head mount of the rug. When we went to bed that night I lay awake a long time wondering about the lobo. Where was it killed? What was the population like in the past? When did these wolves disappear from their historic range? Could there be someone still alive in the area who remembered the lobo? Chabela had told me earlier that she had never seen or heard lobos, but that her dad, Roberto Spence, had talked about them being in this country years ago. I imagined a pack of lobos moving through the oak canyons behind the hacienda, loping across the grasslands hunting. Maybe this area had been a historic wolf run in years past, a natural travel route for lobos moving from the south, crossing La Encantada north to the high country of the Carmens and then east to the Burros.

Mexican lobo rug, 2004

Over the next few years I occasionally thought about the Santo Domingo lobo and studied the slides I had taken. Was it really a lobo? The size of the rug, the gray pelage with black tips, and the large feet did fit the description of a Mexican lobo. I never dreamed that the teeth in the head mount would be important years later.

The Mexican lobo received the same treatment in Mexico as it did in the southwestern United States, that is, it was persecuted to total extirpation. Years later the U.S. Fish and Wildlife Service began a recovery program for the Mexican lobo and sent well-known trapper, Roy Mc-

Bride of Alpine, Texas, to northern Mexico to survey and live capture Mexican lobos for the captive breeding program and later reintroduction of this species into its historic home range. This program has seen many ups and downs; however, Mexican lobos continue to be bred in captivity and several packs are now in the wild in Arizona and New Mexico. There have been no reintroductions in Mexico to date. There are plans and lobos in captivity, but the story is much the same in Mexico as in the southwestern United States. In brief, livestock owners and ranchers don't want the lobo. Perhaps one day vast contiguous lands in northern Mexico can once again support lobos, if sufficient wildlife is available for prey, and if there are still suitable lobos for reintroduction. Many questions remain, and native wildlife populations must be in surplus numbers to support lobos. The biggest factor will be if people in northern Mexico will be willing to coexist with the lobo.

Every story has two sides, and it is understandable that ranchers and ejidos don't want another high-class predator invading their lands and killing livestock. Periodically they have problems to varying degrees with the black bear and puma. Ranchers cannot sustain high losses of livestock to predators, and this is even harder for the ejidos. The ejidos are communally owned properties in which the land is used by many households and each may have only a few goats or other livestock. For ejido residents, every head of livestock is valuable and money from the sale of these animals is their livelihood. In recent years more ranches and a few ejidos are selling hunts for deer, quail, dove, and turkey. The landowners are taking better care of the land and wildlife since its value has increased. Today many ranchers are making more money from hunting revenue than from cattle ranching. So, the lobo may have to wait even longer for releases in Mexico.

In 2001 when I moved to the Carmens, naturally I thought about the Mexican lobo as a species that was once native to this area of northern Coahuila. I also realized that native wildlife numbers were very low in many parts of the region, and that prey numbers were inadequate to sustain even a small pack of lobos in this particular mountain range. In spare moments, I compiled historical information from the borderlands in western Texas and read and reread accounts of lobos in Mexico, looking for references to the lobo here in the Carmens. The only record I could find was the rug at Hacienda Santo Domingo.

Jonás and I had several discussions about this lobo rug, and on one of our trips to Santo Domingo to check telemetry on a couple of elk that had moved into that area, we asked Sam and Jackie Sorrell (Jackie is the daughter of Bobby and Bonnie Paul) if we could photograph the lobo. They said of course, so we took many photos and took hair samples. I was thinking that perhaps we could obtain mtDNA from the hair sam-ples. A few days later I emailed my friend Dave Onorato asking about the DNA from the hair samples. He put me in contact with Robert Wayne at the Conservation Genetics Resource Center, University of California–Los Angeles. Dr. Wayne kindly answered my email saying that the best sample would be a tooth, and could we obtain one? We didn't get a chance to go back to Santo Domingo for a couple of months, and I had to have permission to take the tooth from the head mount in the rug. Bobby Paul gave us permission and Jonás and I returned to Santo Domingo where we very carefully removed a tooth. This took some time and careful scraping and gentle pulling until the tooth finally broke free of the jaw. We sent the tooth to Dr. Wayne, and waited patiently, until October 27, 2004 at 5:30 p.m. when I checked my email and found the note from John Pollinger, director of the Conservation Genetics Resource Center. His email read:

> Sorry [that it] . . . has taken us so long to complete the analysis on the lobo tooth sample. We had to do two extractions to get the DNA and then had to design some new primers to amplify the regions needed to resolve between *Canis lupus lupus* (gray wolf) and *Canis lupus bailey* (Mexican wolf).
>
> The tooth results show that the tooth is definitely from a Mexican wolf. The DNA sequences match up exactly with the Mexican wolf sub-

species (*C. lupus bailey*), and with the studbook Mexican wolf lineage . . . in captivity and now being reintroduced in Arizona and New Mexico by the U.S. Fish and Wildlife Service.

Please let me know if you have further questions regarding the sample or testing. It was a pleasure helping you.

Regards,
John Pollinger

Hacienda Santo Domingo, 2004

The results shown by the DNA sequencing on a sixty-nine-year-old tooth matched the DNA of subspecies *C. lupus bailey*, firmly documenting the presence of this species in the Carmen Mountains in Coahuila. However, the story doesn't end with the DNA analysis. We wanted more information on how the lobo was killed, where exactly it was killed, and by whom. And we had a list of questions pertaining to lobos in general. Time passed, but thanks to Bobby Paul, who contacted a friend of his who remembered the lobo being killed and who killed it, the story continued. We made more phone calls and sent emails. Finally, late in November Bobby tracked down the *vaquero* (cowboy) who killed the lobo.

Victor Coronado, now eighty-eight years old and residing in Acuña, Coahuila, agreed to a visit from us, and said he would tell us about the lobo. Jonás, professional wildlife photographer Patricio Robles Gil, his assistant Jamie Rojo, and I headed to Acuña the next day. It is a six-hour drive from the Carmens to Acuña, so we left early in order to meet Bobby Paul, Jackie Sorrell, and Robert Paul at Ma Crosby's restaurant at 2:00 p.m. On the way we compiled a list of questions, discussed the lobo, and then discussed it again. We met Bobby and family and they showed us the way to Señor Coronado's home. He was sitting on his front porch waiting for us. We quickly introduced ourselves and he remembered Bobby from working on the ranch that Bobby's grandfather owned. He thoroughly enjoyed visiting with us and reminiscing with us about the old days on the big ranches in Coahuila. Victor Coronado worked as a vaquero and later as *caporal* (foreman) for many years for George Miers (Bobby Paul's grandfather) on the San Miguel Ranch and Hacienda Santo Domingo. His memory was incredible, and his eyes sparkled in his weathered face as he recalled riding broncs as a young man. He began telling us about the ranches, the wildlife and of course the lobos. We asked him many questions pertaining to the lobos and he was able to answer all of them. His story of the lobo was quite interesting, and gave us information for the Carmens that we had been lacking on this important carnivore.

He told us that there were never many lobos in the area where he worked and that two lobos were killed in the Santo Domingo area. The first was killed in 1930 by his compadre Juan, and Coronado killed the second one in 1935 in the Álamo pasture. He believed that the one he killed was a male, and it was this 1935 kill that was made into the rug for Santo Domingo. He went on to say that they did not have a regular trapping program for predators, but when they saw coyotes or lobos they would try to shoot them. He said you could always tell the difference between the lobo and the coyote by much larger size, color of the coat (the lobo was always grayish with some black), and much larger tracks. He told us that he knew from conversations with friends years ago that lobos also ranged in La Encantada and the Santa Rosas (surrounding mountains) and that the vaqueros in these mountains shot and trapped them.

Victor said the biggest problem with the lobo was that they killed colts and calves, although they preferred colts. He said the two lobos killed in 1930 and 1935 were the only two he knew of in the Santo Domingo area. He and other cowboys had seen several other lobos in the pastures but did not have the opportunity to shoot them. We asked if he ever heard them howl, he said, "No, never." We also asked him questions about other species of wildlife such as the black bear, grizzly, desert bighorn, pronghorn, bobcat, and coyote. He told us that the black bear, puma, and bobcat were common, but he had never seen or heard of the other species we mentioned in the area. He visited with us several hours and showed us several old photos of vaqueros riding bucking horses and of black bears that were killed on the ranches. It is very important that we record the information from the old-timers since they are the only source of information on many species of wildlife and their presence or absence in years past. When these old-timers are gone, the information goes with them and a part of history is lost forever.

From this interview with Victor Coronado, we can ascertain that perhaps the lobo was not common in this portion of northern Coahuila in the 1930s; their identification was simple because of their size, color, and tracks, and that they killed livestock and preferred colts over calves. Perhaps prior to the late 1800s or early 1900s, the lobo was more common here, but once the large herds of cattle, goats, and sheep infiltrated northeastern Coahuila, landowners began killing predators to prevent depredations on their livestock.

A publication that sheds some light on the distribution of this species in the Carmens is Rollin Baker's *Mammals of Coahuila, Mexico* (1956). Dr. Baker, ninety years young in July 2007 and with a remarkable memory, told me he never saw a specimen of the lobo when he was working in this area. However, Ernest Marsh, who collected plants and some mammals and documented flora and fauna in the Carmen Mountains in the 1930s, told Baker that "wolves were increasing in the Sierra del Carmen and that over 200 cattle were killed in 1934 and 1935 at Santo Domingo by wolves." This conflicts with Victor Coronado's information that lobos were not common and he was working at the Santo Domingo at the time of Marsh's report. Baker also referred to Roberto Spence, a longtime rancher in this area who owned several large ranches northwest of Múzquiz and in the Serranías del Burro. Spence told Baker that in the past thirty years a few lobos were taken in the Piedra Blanca area (east side of the Carmens and west of Santo Domingo), and that in 1953 someone saw wolf tracks in the Serranías del Burro on the Rancho Infante. He went on to say that he doubted that wolves had been numerous since the 1880s when many were trapped because the large flocks of sheep being pastured in the region were preyed on by wolves.

It is fairly easy to imagine a pack of lobos hunting across the broad valley from the Carmens to the Burros; running in the moonlight, tongues lolling, scenting the wind for prey with their supersensitive noses. They belonged here then; and they deserve to be returned to their historic range. However, whether a place for them will be found remains to be seen. Lobos need room, prey, cover, water, denning sites, and a safe environment. Perhaps if large tracts of contiguous lands can be preserved, if native wildlife species numbers reach surplus levels that can support predation, if landowners will coexist with them, and if there are lobos to release, then maybe the Mexican lobo can be returned to its historic range in the Carmens. Maybe again when the night air is cold and the moon hangs like a golden globe in the Coahuila sky, the Mexican lobo will howl his unique melody. Then too, perhaps the mountain will rest, assured that all is well, everything is in balance again.

In April 2006, I had the opportunity to assist with a capture of Mexican lobos at the U.S. Fish and Wildlife Service's Sevilleta Wolf Management Facility in New Mexico. As we prepared to capture the two lobos, a male and a female, I thought how much hardship this species had endured and would probably continue to endure until contiguous large tracts of suitable habitat could be set aside somewhere in the species' historical range where they could once again roam as they did in yesteryear. The capture went smoothly, and while the female was being lifted by many capable hands, the muzzle slipped down from covering her eyes, I found myself staring into the most incredible pair of golden eyes I have ever seen. Hopefully, the day will come when we no longer will be obligated to capture and subject the lobos to being handled, transported, recaptured, and handled again, or placed in pens—when they will once again run free.

3 Chamiceras

The Moreno, Juárez, and Fronteriza Canyons all flow into Cañón el Álamo (also called San Isidro). About a half kilometer from the juncture of the three canyons with El Álamo is a high mountain road that snakes around the forested slopes and canyons of an area known as the *Chamiceras* (loosely, burned place). The morning air was crisp but the sun was rapidly warming the canyon bottom as we headed up the road for my first visit to Chamiceras. The road climbed steadily upward, the vegetation changed rapidly from the lower canyon bottom with its thickets of whitebrush, uña de gato, magueys, and prickly pear, to Mexican pinyon, weeping juniper, and a host of wildflowers and shrubs. I knew this area was reported to have a spectacular waterfall after heavy rains in the higher elevations. Today was my chance to see the waterfall, as last night a rainstorm had pelted the sierras with several inches of rain. The road had been worked recently, enabling us to take the four-wheelers to the top. We bumped along slowly and then crested a high ridge where we stopped to take in the view. Below the crest, the slopes form a huge "∪" sloping downward to Cañón Juárez. The old abandoned Casa Juárez was clearly visible in the morning sun. The arroyo was a winding ribbon of diamond-bright water coming down the canyon where it met with the Arroyo Fronteriza and then flowed into the Álamo. To the east the towering spires of Cañón Temblores were dark purple and red in the morning

Chamiceras waterfall, 2004

light; farther east, the Serranías del Burro were as blue as the Blue Ridge Mountains of Virginia where I grew up. We headed down the other side from the crest entering the oaks with an understory of muhly grasses. The road curved around and opened into a breathtaking meadow with knee-deep pinyon rice grass and pringle grasses, a natural park surrounded by heavily forested steep slopes. The slopes to the east and north were dotted with old silver and lead mines, all now abandoned. A rusted International truck, circa 1940, remains as a reminder of the past. I wondered how the miners got a two-wheel-drive vehicle up this mountain.

The meadow alone is awe-inspiring, and the grasses are lush, the forested slopes a deep emerald green. South on a steep slope a huge rockslide makes a large clear area, and a few ponderosa pines cling precariously to the top of this ridge, silhouetted against a brilliant blue sky. But the true wonder of Chamiceras is not the beauty of this natural meadow or the forest. Just across the canyon, in a maze of sheer red-rock cliffs is a colossal waterfall boiling over the top of a spire, crashing downward with incredible force, snaking over rock overhangs, ending a thousand feet below and disappearing into a thicket of greenery. I could imagine the pool at the base of this cliff—it had to be a churning, swirling mass of water rushing out of the pool and down into the Fronteriza. The rains the night before had created this natural wonder, and it wouldn't last longer than a day or two at the most before trickling to a stop. Then the only reminder of the cascade would be a path carved by the water gushing down the cliff face over the centuries. The sun was quickly heating the air, but still we stood, mesmerized by the falls.

In a smaller canyon complex below, yet another waterfall was shooting out of a rock crevice at the cliff base, but it seemed almost feeble compared to the Chamiceras cataract. The canyons open up and wind back to the north for a short distance coming to an abrupt halt where another series of peaks and cliffs reach upward toward the heavens and the higher elevations of the Maderas at Puerta Linces and Puerta Poblano. Right in the middle of the canyon floor are a small house and water tank made of stone; huge cliffs with jagged peaks seem to stand guard over the lonely little house. I could imagine living here and feeling protected by the mountain sentinels, the gods in a Chihuahuan Desert wonderland.

At another time we were exploring the old mines looking for bat roosts. One mine at the north end of the ridges had been used for many years as a camp for miners and later goat herders. A beat-up iron bed frame, tin cans, a broken wood chair, sotol poles, and other debris littered the mine floor. This mine went gradually deeper into the mountain and also became smaller until we were forced to crawl. We found not a single bat.

Several old tin shacks remain as reminders of the past mining activity. I could well imagine the wind howling and clouds swirling, while the miners hunkered around a wood-burning stove inside the fragile shelters.

On a summer day in 2005, late in the afternoon we decided to check the shacks again for bat roosts. The door was ajar and we gently pushed it open farther so we could squeeze inside while not disturbing roosting bats. The first thing we noticed on the dirt floor was bear scat. I could imagine a bear coming in through the window and exploring the inside of the shack. We began searching the nooks and crannies and rafters in the semi-darkness. We saw it at the same time— either a Townsend's big-eared bat, or a Mexican long-eared bat. We captured it with a hand net, and then photographed and measured it. Sure enough, it was a Mexican long-eared bat, the first time we had documented this species in the Carmens.

There are actually two Chamiceras meadows: the lower one, mentioned previously, and a second opening a short distance upward on a winding game trail. Both meadows are favorite haunts for elk during breeding season. The bulls gather their harem of cows and head for the meadows. Late one afternoon, Jonás, Santiago, and I were in the upper meadow checking radio telemetry signals on the elk, the sun was setting, and dusk was fast approaching. The birds were quiet going to roost, there was no wind, and I remarked how quiet it was. I had hardly uttered the words when a bull elk bugled from the forest above the meadow, and his challenge was answered quickly by a second bull just below us in the lower meadow. Bulls bugling is a sound so primal it gave me goosebumps and stopped me in my tracks. For me, it was a privilege to hear them in this high mountain meadow. We reluctantly picked our way down the path and back to the four-wheelers, listening closely all the while. They only bugled once, but we were content.

Chamiceras is a special place with good memories, hot sunshine, sudden rain storms, and hail so thick on the ground it looked like snow in June. Once, a late snow in April blanketed the spring wildflowers, creating a patchwork of crimson, blue, violet, yellow, and orange on a white quilt. There is always magic here, a place where you feel small when you gaze in all directions, surrounded by towering peaks, distant mountains, churning waterfalls, bear tracks, a sow with three tiny cubs climbing a rock-covered slope, the cubs gamboling along behind her, effortlessly . . .

4 El Club, Home of the Coahuila Mole

Many years ago, El Club was famous for its great hunting opportunities. Hunters from the United States and Mexico made the long trek to the east side of the Carmens to hunt desert mule deer, mountain lions, javelina, Carmen Mountain white-tails, and black bear. This area was a part of a privately owned ranch consisting of about fifty thousand hectares. The property is now owned by Alberto Garza Santos, and the El Carmen Project manages these lands under a conservation agreement.

You would never know that El Club is on the mountain because it is hidden in a complex canyon system on the east side of the Carmens. Just past Ejido Morelos, on the road to La Linda, Coahuila, and the Texas border, a dirt road turns abruptly left and courses across grassland toward majestic peaks. The road winds across the flat passing by the historic Hacienda Piedra Blanca and then turns northwest into the lower canyon country. The vegetation changes from shrub desert to intermittent grasslands to juniper, Mexican persimmon, Mexican redbud, and other woody shrubs as the canyons wind inward and climb gently.

Cañón Botella, 2003

In the distance you see the towering spires called Los Dedos (The Fingers) in the high country. The sheer slopes below Los Dedos are a dense pine and fir forest.

On my first trip to El Club in January 2003 for fieldwork on the baseline inventory project, I was pretty excited about seeing this famous place after hearing about it for many years in Texas and in the stories Dr. Baker told me. Our truck was loaded down with equipment, food, bedrolls, and other paraphernalia, so we were moving slowly along the rutted road, hoping to keep everything intact. Finally, we reached the final gate and entered the El Club area. We had high expectations for this trip, and we were planning to sample small mammals, mist-net birds, collect plants, and look for wintering bats.

El Club was the home of the endemic "Coahuila mole," discovered there by Rollin Baker and his crew in 1951. We had set traps on the west side of the mountain in favorable habitat but had not found the mole. As we drove slowly up the winding driveway to El Club, I was literally drinking in the scenery on both sides of the driveway, a park-like setting of grama and muhlenbergia grasses with a close canopy of oaks and junipers. We arrived at the main camp house, a rock structure that dates from the time when El Club was functioning as a hunting preserve. In years past, this building was the cook shack, with other outbuildings to the west. According to Baker, over the years the other buildings had been destroyed by fire. The cook shack is really a single long room with fireplaces at each end; one end serves as the kitchen and the other a dining and lounging area. A long porch runs across the front of the building and to the left a new building houses the bath.

Below the main rock house, there are two small cabanas constructed of native stone that Alberto Garza had built on the property. We were enthusiastically greeted by Sergio and Clara, part of the El Carmen staff who lived there at that time to caretake the property. Clara is an avid quilter and one of the best cooks in northern Coahuila. We unloaded our groceries and Clara had a fabulous lunch ready for us. After lunch we hurried to the cabanas—the guys took one and I had the other. We unloaded quickly and I spread my sleeping bag, put my gear away, and headed out. I had noted that the cabanas did not have a heat source and it was cold but sunny. Jonás and I baited and set a line of small mammal traps, while Santiago and Feliciano arranged three sets of mist-net poles along the stream in the mouth of Cañón Botella, where we would mist-net birds tomorrow. We finished right at dusk and headed to the cookhouse for hot coffee. Sitting in front of the roaring fireplace, we thawed out while Clara prepared dinner. The radio, which had an antenna made from a wire clothes hanger, was playing *ranchera* music softly in the background. We had a delicious meal and listened to the radio while we talked about the history of El Club. Clara

Los Dedos, El Club. Photo B. P. McKinney, 2010

asked me if I wanted to sleep in the cookhouse since it had a fireplace and thus was warm. I assured her that my sleeping bag was warm and that I would be fine. They headed to their house and we headed to our cabanas.

The moon was up, the canyon was bathed in the light of the full moon, and it was still and frigid. When I went inside my cabana, I quickly realized that it was colder inside than outside. I arranged my sleeping bag and flashlight, and retrieved my journal to write my daily notes. I had brought one last cup of coffee with me. As I snuggled down in the sleeping bag I was thinking about the history of this area, Dr. Baker having worked here many years ago, and I was hoping for good luck trapping. True, it was winter and cold, and maybe nothing was moving. Shortly, I was shivering in the sleeping bag, and the journal notes were finished and so was the coffee. I ventured back outside to the truck and grabbed two extra wool blankets and my long coat, piling these on top of my sleeping bag for more warmth.

I couldn't get comfortable because I was freezing, and finally about 3:00 a.m., I flopped over in bed, and—not realizing how close I was to the bookcase—hit my forehead so hard I saw stars and had tears in my eyes. I got out of the sleeping bag, took two aspirin, and walked outside. The stars were shining, it was cold, and the moonlight was so bright I could see two Carmen Mountain white-tails feeding right below my cabana. Shivering even more, I went back inside and back to the sleeping bag. I finally went to sleep and woke early; by 6:30 I was dressed in layers of clothes and had checked my forehead in the truck mirror, finding a knot the size of an egg. I headed up to the cookhouse anticipating that first cup of coffee. The guys appeared after a few minutes, and as they were too polite to ask how I managed to get the goose egg on my forehead, I finally told them.

After breakfast we headed out to check traps and open mist nets. We were disappointed; we hadn't caught a single small mammal. A beautiful day was in the making—the sky was blue, the sun was slowly warming the canyon, and we were ready to explore. The guys headed up Cañón Botella and I started collecting plants from the cookhouse toward the canyon mouth. The surrounding hills and mountains bear the scars of prolonged overgrazing, with brush so thick you can't walk through it. Vegetation in El Club is in much better shape, thanks to Alberto's buying the property back in the mid-1990s and beginning the resting process of the land. The lower part of the canyon opens below the buildings into a park-like glade dominated by oaks and an understory of native grasses and scattered prickly pear. The mountainsides show scattered juniper, beaked yucca, and grasses with weeping juniper being dominant. Just down the canyon from El Club, the adjoining ranch has a steep-sided mountain covered in brush with a browse line almost at the top of the mountain. I hiked the short distance down to the mouth of the canyon. The riparian area is dominated by alkali sacaton grass, and Godding's willows, madroño, Arizona cypress, pinyon pine, and weeping juniper are abundant on the mountain slopes above the stream.

Cañón Botella is a narrow canyon that comes down from the higher elevations near Campo Uno. This is the main drainage from the high country to the east side of the Carmens. Botella carries an incredible amount of water in times of abundant rainfall in the high country. In January, the water was still swiftly rushing down the canyon over boulders and into deep clear pools. The canyon narrows as it winds upward, and shortly I was faced with a huge boulder pile that blocked my route, so I picked my way over and up and met the guys coming down the arroyo. They had also collected plants, so we stopped and labeled and added them to the press. It was interesting to note that both species of evergreen sumac grow here. We stopped at the last wide pool and set up three nets for bats that night, and a series of trip wires across the pool in hopes of catching some low-flying bats. Naturally we all got soaking wet in the icy stream and were freezing. Santiago leaned over, slipped on a rock, and went head-first into the creek. It was time to go to the cookhouse for coffee, and so we headed back down the canyon and to headquarters, on the way stopping to set four one-hundred-meter long vegetation transects so that we could begin monitoring vegetation in this area over a period of time. As we were walking up the driveway we saw a pair of golden eagles circling high above Botella. Once we reached the camp and warmed up, we pulled out the spotting scopes and located the much-used bulky stick nest of the golden eagles, which was high in a rock overhang on the cliff. At about 7:30 p.m. we unfurled the nets, but luck was not with us—no wintering bats were out that night. We closed the nets at 11:00 p.m. and headed to the cookhouse to warm up by the fireplace. Despite the cold, I slept all night.

The next morning we had a white-ankled mouse in the traps and mist-netted a few dark-eyed juncos and one American robin. We collected more plants up the Botella. I was disappointed. Where was Baker's mole? Our gopher traps had yielded nothing. I dreaded going back and emailing Doc that we hadn't caught the famous Coahuila mole. The wind picked up and the clouds were blue-black and rolling over the mountains. Mist-netting bats in the high wind was impossible. We called it an early day and after dinner headed to our cabanas. I added birds to our growing list, noting that nothing unusual had been ob-

served. Common birds were canyon, spotted and green-tailed towhees, black-crested titmice, dark-eyed juncos, robins, Mexican jays, ruby-crowned kinglets, several Audubon's orioles that are resident species, rock and canyon wrens, and both mountain and western bluebirds. There was a noted absence of wintering sparrows, with only a few savannah sparrows feeding alongside the resident black-throated and rufous-crowned sparrows. I kept reminding myself that this was just a preliminary trip to get to know the area, and that it was January, the middle of winter.

The next day would be our last day in the field before we headed back to the Los Pilares headquarters on the west side. The morning was cold and windy with dark clouds moving in over the mountain, which was not good weather for fieldwork. We caught two species of mice: a white-ankled and a deer mouse. We made study skins with freezing hands and established two more vegetation transects, and then hiked up the west canyon collecting plants. We all watched the golden eagles at sunset and Feliciano and I closed the mist nets, while Santiago and Jonás were occupied taking photos of the full moon rising over the cliffs. The clouds had blown out and the night was cold and windy. We compiled our lists and wrote field notes and called it a day. I went outside later when the wind had died down; I was glad to be here even if the trip wasn't a resounding success for collecting and finding the Coahuila mole. The full moon hung over the cliffs, which were jet black in the shadows and seemed to tower upward for miles. It was so quiet that all I could hear was my own breathing.

The next day was hectic. We pulled trap lines—only one deer mouse. We rolled nets, packed the truck, prepared one final study skin, and then a photo session to top it all. We wanted to send Doc Baker lots of photos of El Club some fifty years after he was there last. We reached our headquarters at Los Pilares on the other side of the mountain around 3:30 p.m. and unloaded equipment. We already had our second trip planned.

Our second trip to El Club began on April 16, 2003. Surely this time we would catch the Coahuila mole and be able to email Doc Baker that yes, this species was still there and doing well. If you are wondering why this species is so important, Baker and his crew collected the first specimen here at El Club on February 28, 1951, and the species has not been reported since that time. The Coahuila mole is endemic to the Maderas del Carmen, and the only information on this species derived from the single specimen collected in 1951. We left Los Pilares around noon; the truck was piled with equipment lashed on, it was warm, and dust was blowing. We reached El Club about 3:00 p.m. Jonás, Feliciano, and I began unloading with Sergio and Clara pitching in to help. We stowed all of our gear in the two cabanas and decided to work the canyon that ran northwest from camp. Sergio and Jonás found a mottled rock rattler. We set three long mist nets criss-crossing the canyon over pools of water, hoping for a good bat flight.

That night was cold with a little wind. While we were waiting for dusk, Sergio told us he found a bobcat skull, which he gave us for the mammal collection. He then brought forth the snout of a subadult black bear. He said a nearby rancher had killed the bear and sent us the snout, and that the bear had been killing calves. At dusk we filled the thermos with coffee and headed up the canyon to open mist nets. We set up our data station up on the tailgate of the pickup. The wind was variable for several hours; the bats would fly when it was still and quit flying when the wind picked up, which was normal. We had good luck even in the cool temperatures and wind, as we caught five species. At 11:30 p.m., the temperature was dropping rapidly, and we were shivering with wet feet and so sleepy we could hardly keep our eyes open. We all got inside the truck and started the heater to warm up, Feliciano promptly fell asleep and began snoring. We closed and furled the nets at 1:00 a.m. and headed to the cabanas. We had caught a good mix: hoary bats, a ghost-faced bat, Brazilian freetails, western pipistrelle, and cave myotis—not bad for a cold windy night. The birds we observed that day were mostly the common resident species, but we had added sharp-shinned and common black hawk, white-throated swift, common poor-will and whip-poor-will, black phoebe, canyon wren, and western screech owl to our growing list of birds for the area.

Wild turkeys walking on the tin roof of the cabana woke me early the next morning. They then decided to have a gobbling contest in front of the cabana, so there was no sleeping late. Never have I heard four gobblers make so much noise. They alternated strutting and gobbling on the roof, and then flying to the grassy area in front of the cabana and repeating the process.

We ran the mammal trap lines early; all the traps were empty so we began working up the voucher specimens of the bats we had collected the night before. Jonás skinned and I mounted the specimens, which improved our efficiency. We hiked up the north canyon, which we call Cañón Club, and saw two lizards sunning on the rocks. Before we could identify them, they scrambled into the rock pile. Later we hiked down to Botella and caught an eastern black-necked garter snake, which we photographed and released. We finished up the field notes that afternoon and added the northern saw-whet owl that we heard calling the night before.

The evening looked very good for bat netting, as it was cloudy, the moon was covered, and little or no wind. We headed out to Cañón Club at dusk and unfurled the nets. Bats were flying early, and we began capturing them immediately. We had three nets out and three people, so each of us worked a net. We caught pallids, western pipistrelles, Brazilian freetails, many hoary bats, Yuma myotis, big brown bat, California myotis, and long-legged myotis.

At about 10:00 p.m., the flight slowed down and we were working up the captured bats, taking measurements and weight and periodically checking the nets. Jonás left to check the nets and returned quickly, saying, "This is a new species." We had a Mexican long-nosed bat, a new species for the bat inventory, and it was very important to document it here. This species is sooty brown colored with a long nose and prominent nose-leaf. The tail is minuscule and the general impression is that the bat has no tail. This is a colonial species and migratory; it is rarely seen in western Texas, being documented only from the Chisos Mountain in Big Bend National Park and west in the Chinati Mountains in Presidio County. Although this bat occurs in many areas of Mexico, it is relatively sparse over most of its range. There are indications that the population may be declining. Nectar and pollen are the main foods in these bats' diet, and they are believed to migrate north in response to the blooming period of the magueys. When the maguey flowers open at night, the bats feed on the pollen and nectar, moving from one plant to the next, thus cross-pollinating the plants. Both the plants and the bats benefit from the relationship. This dependence is so strong that in some cases plants cannot propagate without the help of the bats.

With renewed energy we were back to checking nets and the bats were flying. I walked up the creek to the farthest net and to my dismay found the net down in the creek; the whole bottom shelf was ripped completely and one hoary bat was caught in the top shelf, which was draped over a boulder. Wading into the creek in the mud, I yelled for Jonás to help me reset the net. While I was waiting I removed the bat from the net and put him in a cloth bag to wait his turn to be measured and weighed. Jonás arrived and we started to raise the net. At the same time we saw a gray-banded kingsnake slither across the rocks; we dropped the net and began digging in the rocks in the creek to try and catch it. By this time we were both wet and muddy and the snake was long gone. We finally just took the net down and bagged it, full of leaves and twigs.

Going back across the creek using my headlight for guidance, I slipped on a rock and fell, getting completely covered in water and mud. We furled the nets at 1:30 a.m. On the way back to camp, we were talking about the gray-banded kingsnake, as this was the third one we had seen in the Maderas. The three we had observed were all in riparian habitat: one at Campo Uno around two thousand meters elevation, one in Cañón el Álamo at a *tinaja* (watering hole or water-filled basin in rocks) in the arroyo, and the third here at El Club in streamside habitat. Being very familiar with gray-banded kingsnakes since I lived on the Black Gap Wildlife Management Area for many years, I couldn't believe their presence here because the habitat was so different. In West Texas in the Big Bend, Rosillos, and Black Gap, the gray-banded kingsnakes inhabit the dry rock shelves in canyons and low desert habitat, whereas here they were in the oak woodlands in riparian habitat and they were beautiful with bright orange

saddles. Another species that I had believed we would find in the Carmens was the Trans-Pecos copperhead, but so far no luck.

The next few days were repeats of the previous days, depending on the weather. On April 18, we contended with cold wind all day, so we moved the specimen preparation inside the camp house. At about 5:30 p.m., the wind finally died down; it was still cloudy but the temperature had warmed up considerably. We hurried to move nets and set up in the lower Botella. By 9:30 p.m., it was sprinkling rain but the bats were flying. We caught only one new species, an eastern pipistrelle, and we captured more of the ever present hoary bats. They are one of the most common species in the Carmens from the lower elevations to the high pine-fir forests. Around 1:00 a.m. we furled the nets and headed to the camp house for peanut butter sandwiches and coffee. I was lying awake at 2:00 a.m. listening for owls and wondering why we were not hearing elf owls in this area. I had not heard a single one on either side of the mountain in any type of habitat, and they should be here. I remembered Ro Wauer recorded them in the Carmens back in 1969.

On our last field day, April 19, we checked traps and found nothing. What a disappointment. Where was the Coahuila mole? We prepared voucher specimens all day and put out nets again tonight at Botella, catching only hoary bats and a couple of myotis. The wind picked up and was howling down the canyon, so we furled the nets and called it a night. Early the next morning we started pulling trap lines, taking down nets, and packing the truck. The specimens were pinned to Styrofoam sheets and we had these balanced on top of equipment boxes in the back seat of the truck along with Feliciano. The front seat was full of notebooks and more specimens and the back of truck had equipment lashed on. We headed out about noon and as we were climbing the Cuesta Malena to cross to the other side of the Carmens, we saw a Mexican racer in the road. We all jumped out and started chasing the snake who wanted nothing more than to escape. Jonás finally caught him after falling down in the middle of the road just as he reached for the snake. We had thus far not been able to catch this species, even though we had seen several in the low and mid elevations on the west side of the Carmens. We had to do some innovative equipment rearranging to find a cloth bag in which to keep the racer so that we could photograph it later.

All things considered, it was a great trip, with new bat species and the racer, but still no Coahuila mole. I was wondering if we were ever going to find one. We had checked gopher runs, dug up suspicious-looking mounds of dirt, placed traps everywhere, and still no luck. We briefed Sergio before leaving El Club on exactly what to look for and were hoping he would at least catch a glimpse of one since he was there for weeks every month. We planned another trip for the fall and hoped to have better luck then.

On October 26, 2003, about mid-morning Sergio called on the radio from El Club and said he had caught a funny little animal that he thought might be the "topo de Coahuila." We were excited, with the three of us trying to talk at the same time on the radio. At the time, a gangly youth named Chuy who had big hands was working for us at El Carmen. Sergio described the animal saying that he was gray, had no eyes, and his feet were like Chuy's hands—definitely a mole. We gave him explicit directions on how to wrap it up and put it in the small freezer on the gas refrigerator. Then I worried that he would run out of butane, the skin would be ruined, and so forth.

Two days later Sergio and Clara drove in to Los Pilares with the little animal they caught. Sure enough, it was the Coahuila mole, and finally, after a forty-two-year hiatus, we had the second one known to science from the same general location where Baker and his team had collected the first one in February 1951. We took dozens of photos and I sent emails to everyone I knew, but the first went to Doc Baker and the second to Clyde Jones. Jonás carefully skinned it and I mounted it. He did a marvelous skinning job, and this little one was the best mount that I had ever worked up. We were so careful. I was very worried that we wouldn't get perfect results. Suppose the scalpel slipped, or suppose I pulled a thread too tight and ripped the skin. But luck was with us, and the specimen worked up nicely.

What an amazing and secretive creature this

mole is. We still know very little about this species living on a sky island in Coahuila. We need information on its life history and population information. Basically, we are familiar with the habitat, we know they are rare, and we have measurements for two specimens. Perhaps in subsequent years we will be able to spend more time learning about this secretive species. In his response to my email, Doc Baker wrote that some of his colleagues over the years were skeptical, but now there was proof! Sergio was correct: the mole did have feet like Chuy's hands.

In the summer of 2004, Sergio again called on the radio to report that he had caught a funny-looking snake. The description he gave us over the radio had us wondering what it could be—with no reference to Chuy, we were lost. In a couple of days we traveled to El Club, and learned that Sergio had scored again. I teased the biologists—what did I need them for? Sergio was bringing in the records; maybe I should just elevate his job definition to wildlife technician. Sergio had caught a Trans-Pecos copperhead, the first recorded for the Carmens. We had not found a single one on the west side of the mountain. I had been thinking that perhaps the east side was more diverse in some ways, that we might find species there we hadn't recorded on the west side. Two species—the Coahuila mole and now the Trans-Pecos copperhead—were pointing in that direction.

A year later in August 2005, Clyde Jones and wife Mary Ann (two of my favorite people in the world), David Riskind, Jim Hendrickson, and Jesus V. Reyna visited El Carmen for a week. I was in the field when they arrived but hurried to headquarters. Amid the hellos and hugs, I said, "Wait until you see the Coahuila mole!" Clyde informed me that he had already found it. He couldn't wait on me, and simply walked into the office, pulled the mammal collection, and checked it out.

No matter how many new species we find over the years in the Carmens, I do not believe that any will compare with the re-documenting of the Coahuila mole.

Coahuila mole, 2003

Our schedule had been so busy that we couldn't find time to go to Mesa Bonita, even though this was an area I was very anxious to visit. Jonás knew the area well because his master's degree was focused on the diet of black bears here in the Carmens and he had filled my head with visions of what this high mountain mesa looked like. I was ready to see it for myself. Finally, on July 12, 2002, we had a full day planned for the sierra. It had been raining non-stop for a week, and on that day we had sunshine and hot weather. We packed two of the Kawasaki Mules (four-wheel-drive utility vehicles, known as *mulas*) with our equipment. Plant collecting was the agenda for the day. Jonás and I were in one mula and Feliciano and Santi were in the second. We were loaded with plant presses, notebooks, clippers, collection bags, field guides, cameras, lunches, and various other types of equipment. We headed out early, the mulas slowly grinding up the mountain.

Coming down the canyon from our house to Pilares, I had seen two bears earlier in the day and thought we would probably see more in the higher country. They were feeding on the ripe fruits and lush grasses and highly visible. Slowly we made our way upward, finally arriving at El Cinco. We turned left and headed upward to Campo Dos. The drive from Campo Cinco to Campo Dos is beautiful, as there is tremendous diversity in plant life and you gradually move from the pine-oak forest to pine-fir forest.

We reached Campo Dos and unloaded our equipment, had lunch, and put all the plants we had collected in the presses and labeled the sheets. Plant collecting in the sierra is a rich experience because of the diversity—yucca and pine, dogwood, basswood, orchids, wild roses, agaves, succulents, firs, grasses and cactus, and hundreds of wildflowers all in bloom, and all in a high evergreen woodland. Water was rushing down all the

Aspen tree at Mesa Bonita, 2002

creeks, crystal clear and cold as ice in July. In some places we were barely able to ford with the mulas. We passed a stand of three quaking aspen. This is not a common species here; only three stands are known.

Upon leaving Dos, we headed left up the mountain. The road turned into a boulder-strewn alley in the middle of a tight canyon. This is actually where Cañón Oso starts, but more about that canyon later. The water was rushing down what used to be the road as if it were the creek bed, when meanwhile the creek on the left was also rushing. One place was so rocky that I was holding my breath, holding the dashboard with the one hand and equipment in the middle of the seat with the other. As Jonás eased the mula over the rocks, water was eddying on the floorboard. We made it up and the road cleared somewhat. I looked back just as Feliciano crossed himself with Santi hanging on for dear life as they started up the boulder-strewn road. They made it through as well, the going became smoother, and up and up we climbed.

What an incredibly lush wild forest, with plants growing everywhere, and ferns growing out of rocks and alongside the creek banks. Painted redstarts were flitting around the trees, and their red, black, and white plumage was a striking contrast to the greens of vegetation. The ever-present Mexican jays were screaming their displeasure as we invaded their territory, and acorn woodpeckers were swooping from tree to tree.

We passed the sign to Campo Tres, which was on our agenda for later in the day. But first the Mesa Bonita.

We made another really steep climb, and were barely inching along up the grade. We topped out and the mountain opened into a meadow that was part of the mesa. The view atop the mountain is truly awesome. The meadow was covered in grasses, and with the abundant rains, many areas had become marshes. Water continually squished up over our boots while we walked around exploring. There were bear scratches on many of the trees, and turned-over logs where they had searched for insects. Many pocket gopher tunnels were observable, and tufted titmice and white-breasted and pygmy nuthatches were flitting from tree to tree.

This area had burned years ago; old burned trees remained, but the regrowth was impressive. There were large stands of ponderosa pine and oaks, with the ponderosa being the dominant large tree. This area had also been logged extensively and there were piles of old stacked wood. We collected plants and headed up to the lookout point, called El Mirador. Clouds were building fast and the temperature was dropping; although it was July, it was getting cold really fast. We drove slowly upward on an old logging road, parked the mulas, and hiked over to the edge of the cliff. By this time we were cloud covered. Literally walking in the clouds, we could hear a waterfall close by, which was curious given that we were standing on the mountain top on flat ground. Where was the sound coming from? Peering over the edge of the cliff, I saw the tops of giant fir trees. We could see into the far distance, even amid the eddying mist of clouds. Birds had ceased singing. The only sounds were the wind in the pines and the waterfall. We looked down to our left where yet another waterfall was spurting out of the rocks, not the large one crashing nearby, but a second one.

Then, literally at the same moment, we saw the *chichimoco* (cliff chipmunk), scampering about on the boulders right in front of the small waterfall. This was our first sighting, and there was no way that could we reach him or even get to that area to set a live trap. The chichimoco is a little guy, gray in color with dark cinnamon dorsal stripes, short legs, and a fluffy tail. He wasn't the least bit interested in us, but seemed to have his own agenda that didn't include climbing up to where we were. We watched him until he scampered out of sight in the vegetation near the waterfall. The cliff chipmunk is found in several locales in Mexico, but the subspecies *Eutamias dorsalis carminis* (Goldman 1951) is restricted in range. This is another species unique to the Carmens.

We hiked straight down the side of a cliff to the second waterfall, and it was nothing short of amazing. Water was literally running across a flat mesa, and then pouring down a rock chute, crashing over boulders where the spray was cold.

Chichimoco (cliff chipmunk).
Photo J. D. Villalobos, 2002

Climbing back up the cliff required a one-step-up-and-three-back routine because the ground was slippery. We scrambled to the top and hiked back to El Mirador. The clouds had suddenly lifted and the view below was breathtaking. At our left, we could see the east side of Pico Centinela, and below a chasm, spread out in a wide, steeply sloped, heavily forested canyon system ending up at El Club. At our right, the spires of the *dedos* rose skyward. Far out on the flats, the Ejido Morelos was visible. To the northeast, the jagged peaks of Pico Etero near La Linda, Coahuila, were visible, and farther still, the limestone cliffs in Maravillas Canyon on the Black Gap Wildlife Management Area. These were the very peaks I saw years ago from Black Gap. At that time, I never dreamed I would be living in these moun-

tains. I had flown over this area recording black bear and desert bighorn sheep telemetry, but I never imagined this landscape. Aerial and ground perspectives are a world apart. I never considered the possibility that this high mountain mesa was truly a mesa and a marsh, a ponderosa pine park, a haven for birds and other wildlife, and home to the famous chichimoco.

This area is also the only place in the Carmens where the quaking aspen makes a stand. The three trees mentioned previously on the road to Dos are at the lowest elevation. Here there is a large stand on a ridge to the southeast of El Mirador, and across the canyon there is also a large stand tucked up in a narrow canyon in El Jardín. The fall color on the quaking aspens provides a bright gold splash in the landscape of dark green pines and the golds, reds, and oranges of oaks and maples.

Later we found many chichimocos and caught several in small mammal traps. This is another species for which little is known about the ecology; they inhabit canyons in the mountains from around two thousand meters to the highest elevations of over 2,700 meters. The largest population is found near the road to Pico Loomis, the highest point in the Carmens. The Carmens mark the northern-most occurrence of this species in Coahuila. Baker (1956) reported that acorns seemed to be a favorite food and caches were stored under ledges.

We headed down the mountain, and then

turned left toward Campo Tres, another logging camp of yesteryear. Nothing prepared me for what I would see at Campo Tres. The soil changes from dark black loam to red clay on this high ridge. We bumped along the washed-out road, fording creeks and newly formed arroyos full of water. Suddenly after a short climb, you are faced with an incredible view of a three-story-high stack of cut and uncut lumber surrounded by deep sawdust. Over the years, bears had tunneled underneath—what a perfect place for a bear to hibernate. The logs and planks of the lumber tower are silver with age and some are rotting. So many trees cut, hauled in, and left lying in a titanic heap. What a waste. It would be impossible to burn this stacked quantity of lumber, as the fire danger would be too great to risk. Hauling it all off the mountain would also be impossible. Perhaps in hundreds of years it will slowly decompose, although I seriously doubt that it will happen in that time frame. Meanwhile, bears can use it to hibernate, insects can make homes providing food for woodpeckers and flickers, and small rodents and other mammals can use it for cover and nesting.

A small sluggish stream flows at the base of the stack of lumber. The water is orange, a by-product of the tannic acid from the lumber leaching into the stream. Little vegetation grows here. Across the stream and up a slope, there is a small meadow and an old lumber camp. A wood shack and some loose tin are all that remain. We ex-plored the meadow, collected plants, and had almost reached the mulas when we saw the bear. He didn't wind us, so we crept closer under the cover of the pines, and for about thirty minutes we watched him feeding on the succulent grasses and horsetails in a little clearing below the stack of lumber. Being a bear, he was intently focused on feeding with little regard for anything else. We were able to take some great photos of the bear standing knee deep in green grass. Eventually the wind changed and he huffed and ran off, disappearing into the thick forest. He was the third bear I had seen that day and I was hoping to see more on the way down the mountain.

We climbed into the mulas and headed down the mountain to Campo Dos where the plant presses and equipment were loaded and we headed down the mountain for Los Pilares. We had just passed Los Cojos, an abandoned mine site, and I remarked that we "never see any bears here." Naturally, wildlife always makes a liar out of a person. Immediately we saw a sow with two small cubs amble across the road in front of us. She and the cubs dropped down into a small arroyo and then climbed back up onto the road behind us. We quickly turned around and headed back; luckily we were able to get one photo of her and the cubs before she disappeared into the brush. Feliciano and Santi missed her completely since they were a ways behind us. Six bears in one day, I thought, not bad. This was one of my best days in the Carmens. The mesa, the chichimoco, birds, new plants, breathtaking views, and six bears—I didn't want the day to end. I can never have enough days in the field, but a day like this one was perfection. To end this grand field day, we were gifted with a blazing red, orange, and purple sunset. As we came off the mountain, the cliffs were bathed in multihued colors, while far to the west the sun was setting behind the mountains in Chihuahua. I drove slowly home to Casa San Isidro contemplating my good fortune.

6 El Jardín and Cañón del Diablo—Peregrine Palaces

For many years I had heard of El Jardín. I knew it was somewhere in the Carmens on the east side, and that it had been famous among hunters in the United States who journeyed there to hunt black bear and Carmen Mountain white-tailed deer. I had conjured up many images, but really had no idea of what El Jardín was really like. On one of my first trips to the CEMEX El Carmen Project area, we made a trip to El Jardín to carry supplies to a crew working there on water lines. We left the old Los Pilares headquarters on the west side of the mountain late one March afternoon in 2001. The sky was dark and the wind was up. I mentioned that I thought it might storm but everyone assured me that it probably would not. There is no passable road from the west to the east side on the mountain. We had to drive up through the Cuesta Malena, and then down the other side to El Melón, where we then turned north, heading in the direction of La Linda and the Texas border.

I was excited—finally, I was going to see the famed El Jardín. The road was rough and the going slow. I had plenty of time to drink in the landscape and make notes on the birdlife. Finally, we reached the Pila de Agua Chile, and turned off onto the road that would eventually take us to El Jardín via a ranch and other private lands. We stopped briefly at the Agua Chile ranch and visited with a vaquero, and then headed on into the canyon.

The road winds gradually upward; it is rough and requires four-wheel drive in most parts. Spring wildflowers were just beginning to pop up along the roadside and in the grassland. Stewart's gilia, paperflower, Texas vervain, Dakota vervain, Indian paintbrush, desert baileya, and a host of other wildflowers dotted the landscape. The air was cold, coming directly from the north and the dark clouds continued building. They were literally boiling up and over Pico Centinela. I again remarked that it sure looked like it was going to storm, and again the reply was, "looks more like wind than rain." Suddenly, a bolt of lightning shattered the sky and jagged downward. We'll see, I thought to myself. I was also happy that I had brought my long drover coat with the sheepskin lining.

We topped out on a limestone ridge after bumping up a series of rock shelves; the odor of dogweed was pungent, a smell that always reminds me of limestone rock and desert country. Below us, an arroyo wound down through a canyon, where a few relic cottonwoods remained. We snaked downward and into the dry arroyo. Birds were sparse here, but maybe they were preparing for the approaching storm. Mourning doves flushed from the brush along the bank of the arroyo, and canyon towhees, rock wrens, cardinal, phainopepla, and pyrrhuloxia were common.

The routine was a slow climb, grinding upward toward the summit, then easy going for a few miles, and then back down into the arroyo. A cold wind was still blowing out of the north, and the thunder and lightning were closer and more frequent. I could smell rain on the wind. The storm was fast approaching and looked like it was going to be a dandy. We made one more climb up through the grasslands, dropped down into the arroyo and up the other side. There were two old buildings, one an abandoned house that was minus windows and doors, the other a long, narrow, whitewashed adobe building that the caretaker and his wife lived in. Farther north a short distance, there was an old set of corrals and a *pila* (aboveground water tank). Just as the truck rolled to a stop all hell broke loose. Sheets of rain, wind, thunder, and lightning—the fury of the mountain weather system was upon us. The storm raged for thirty minutes or so and blew down the canyon and out across the valley toward the Serranías del Burro. Meantime, we had been huddled in the truck watching the sheets of rain and water running everywhere. I opened the truck door and was hit with an icy blast of air. Stepping down, I sank into the mud, and after pulling one foot out I gingerly tiptoed across the mud toward the caretaker's house. We all went inside and Martin's wife was busy making coffee and tortillas, much to my delight. After coffee and dinner, it was pitch dark and the wind was howling. Another storm was building. About 9:00 p.m., we tiptoed back across the mud to the little house with no windows and doors. We unloaded cots and sleeping bags with the aid of a single flashlight. Bill and I took the back room of the two-room house. The other guys took the front room, which had no door. We arranged our sleeping bags and cots and headed to bed. Around 10:00 p.m. the second storm hit, and I thought that little white adobe house was going to be lifted off the hill and dropped into the arroyo. I was pretty comfortable in my sleeping bag with my big coat on top of it. Billy Pat said, "The roof is leaking." I answered, "Well, not where I am." He moved his cot, and shortly I felt a very cold spot on my feet, and discovered I too was under a drip. I moved my cot, we kept this up for some time, inching our cots farther across the room until there was no more room. We found a bucket to put under the big drips. Finally, all was quiet. I was kinda scrunched up to avoid the drip but warm and comfortable.

The wind was shrieking, the rain was pelting down on the old tin roof, and I was thinking of the towering peaks we saw coming in. The firs and pines were probably bending nearly double with the force of the wind. The arroyos would be starting to run water downward to the desert grasslands. Birds and wildlife would be hunkered down in the shelter of brush, rocks, and caves to avoid the storm. I was slowly drifting off to sleep when I was shocked awake by howling and screeching and the guys in the front room yelling in Spanish and stumbling around. About that time the banshee creature entered our room, where it bounced off my cot, then onto Billy Pat's, and finally into the corner of the room. The "banshee" turned out to be a scared feral housecat, and poor Homero was still stumbling around in the dark wondering what had attacked him. The cat apparently had claimed the old house for his own. He jumped up on the first cot and landed squarely on Homero's head, and then moved on to more intruders. We finally got the cat outside and everyone back in bed. By then it was 1:30 a.m. The storm died down and I snuggled down in the sleeping bag one more time.

Daylight came quickly, it seemed. We were up and ready for coffee early. The wood smoke smelled wonderful. I have always associated wood smoke, particularly *huisache* (sweet acacia), with Mexico. A clean sweet smell that signals a new day or the evening cooking fire, its fragrance tugs at my inner self.

We hurried over to the cook house and morning coffee was never so good. It was cold, but the sky was clear. After breakfast we doubled up on the four-wheelers and headed out to explore the area above the camp and up to Cañón del Diablo.

I had heard about this canyon years ago from a friend in West Texas, who said, "Well, it is something else—I would rather stand on top of Diablo than the Grand Canyon." The wind was freezing cold but the sun came up shortly and started warming up the country. We muddled around in a series of old roads that were literally going in circles. Nine old trucks in various stages of rust and decrepitude dating from the 1950s had been abandoned at different locations along the roads. All had numbers smeared in white paint. After passing number nine for the third time, we decided that we were taking a wrong turn somewhere. This area, which had not been overgrazed, is a high mountain grassland surrounded by forest of ponderosa and oak; higher on the slopes the firs are dominant. Finally, we reached the Diablo summit and the view truly was astounding. We were standing on top of the world, where we could see for miles and miles to the north, including Black Gap, Big Bend, Santiago Peak, the Rosillos, Persimmon Gap, and Nine Point Mesa in West Texas. Due west, the top of Pico Cerdo (Schott Tower) appeared to be literally hanging in the air, suspended off to the side of the escarpment. The canyon system itself is an incredible maze of arroyos running this way and that but connecting in one way or another. Far below mammoth limestone cliffs was bright green vegetation in the canyon bottom; perhaps there was a spring below. This huge canyon complex actually drains on both sides of the mountain, which I had dubbed El Jardín East and El Jardín West. The east side, where we were standing that day, eventually drains out toward the former Adams Ranch, also a conservation area currently owned by CEMEX USA and the Cuenca Los Ojos Foundation. The west side drains through a tight canyon onto the sandy soils south of Boquillas del Carmen near the Ejido Jaboncillos, where it empties into a wide arroyo that runs directly to the Rio Bravo

del Norte. This is the Sierra del Carmen in all her glory, extending to the border and entering West Texas near the boundary of the Big Bend National Park and the Adams Ranch, now called El Carmen Land and Conservation Company LLC. Texas maps identify the high ridges as the Sierra del Carmen and the Sierra Caballo del Muerto (Dead Horse Mountains).

But my eyes kept returning to the cliffs. The guys wandered off and I started searching the immense cliff faces for peregrine eyries. I had chased peregrine falcons in West Texas for seventeen years, and seen this country from the air, and now here I was right on the ground, right on the rim of the canyon. In just minutes I heard a falcon screech the familiar, "kak, kak, kak." I found the falcon sitting in her eyrie, gazing over her vast domain. I watched the tiercel come in and then leave. It was quiet, the wind down, and the sun warm.

I was reminded of my first trip to the Carmens via helicopter to chase peregrines. It was a spring day in the Black Gap and I was so excited that I could barely stand still. I was waiting on my ride to finally go to the big cliffs in the Carmens and spend a day and a half looking for peregrines. I hefted the heavy, faded green pack from my truck and went over my list one more time. I couldn't afford to forget anything since the helicopter would drop me off this afternoon and return midmorning tomorrow to pick me up. I was anxious, ready to go. I paced the dirt landing strip where

Cañón del Diablo. Photo J.D. Villalobos, 2006

Sierra del Carmen escarpment. Photo J. D. Villalobos, 2006

the pilot would set the chopper down. Finally, I hear the flat whop-whop of the rotor blades and see the chopper coming in low and fast over the desert hills.

The pilot was a friend—he and I had worked peregrines before, and I trusted him for canyon and mountain work. He set the big machine down, creating a mini-dust storm. I grabbed my pack and a gear bag and staggered through the dust to the chopper. Quickly I stowed the gear and returned for my scope pack and small ice chest. He popped the other door open and I climbed in, grabbing for the headset, settling down, and hooking the safety belt all in one smooth motion. I was ready to go. He grinned and asked if I were ready. I gave him the thumbs up and said, "Let's turn and burn." He knows I love helicopters and how excited I was about the trip. His grin widened as he replied, "Let's rock and roll." We lifted off and I felt the heat from the sun warm on my face as we gained altitude. There was not a cloud in the sky. The country slid by below, greens and browns like in a wet watercolor. We climbed steadily. I talked to him through the headset, giving him explicit directions. We head south. The greenbelt of vegetation in an otherwise brown landscape alerted us that we were crossing the river into Mexico.

I tell him that I believe that the best approach to the peak I need to be on will be to go behind the low rims, climb into the high country of the Carmens, and then turn back sharply to the northeast to reach the high peak. "Okay," he says, his radio crackling in my ear. I draw a deep breath. The escarpments can only be described as a natural miracle. I grin and then decide to share my thought with him. "Hey, a friend of mine in Mexico would say, 'Es un milagro.'" He nods in agreement, "This is an incredible sight, it is really something else." I tell him to fly just a little more west, and then turn back north and that should line us up perfectly with the peak. He knows I need to be as close to the edge as I can get, and that I can't hike far with three heavy packs and an ice chest.

We turn north and I feel the excitement building inside me; my throat is dry, my hands icy. We slow and begin searching for a spot to land where the tail rotor will not encounter tall vegetation. We zig and jig—he calls it maneuvering in position—between dead bloom stalks of sotol and maguey plants. He sets the chopper down gently, testing the ground. Perfect as usual. I strip off the headset, he cuts the motor, and we wait until the rotors stop. We jump out and he helps me unload. He looks around to make sure I haven't forgotten anything.

"You have everything?" he asks.

"Yep, and I have my radio. Guess I better try it." I punch in the tower button and hear the Black Gap tower open.

"Seventeen fifty-three to seventeen fifty-one," I say.

The radio crackles and my husband's voice

comes in loud and clear, "Go ahead, seventeen fifty-three."

"We are on the ground, just checking my radio."

"You are coming in loud and clear. Call in tonight."

"Okay, ten-four."

I turn and with a grin, say, "See you tomorrow and thanks for putting me in the perfect place."

"Great, see you in the morning."

He heads to the waiting chopper and I lug the packs a little farther away. The engine turns and the rotors start a slow whirl, and then faster and faster until they are a blur of motion. He lifts the chopper up and sideways, literally falling off the cliff. I chuckle. The whop-whop of the blades fades and I want to dance with joy.

First things first, I remind myself. I hustle, unpacking the gear bag and setting up my small tent, a vivid blue reminder of the modern world. It is out of place on this ancient mountain. I choose a spot on the south side of two sotol plants. The bright green plants will break the force of the wind. The silence is tangible. I hurry, anxious to get to work.

I methodically set up camp, water jug in the shade along with the ice chest, and sleeping bag, flashlight, and clock in the tent. I zip the tent to keep out creepy crawlers. Food is minimal, but there is always good coffee. My coffee pot, cup, crackers, boiled eggs, pickles, and apples make up the rest. I flip open my small shovel and hastily dig a small fire ring. I line it with rocks and rustle up some small pieces of wood. I don't need much, just enough to make coffee. I stand, hands on my hips, and survey my camp. It will do: I've had better and worse.

I unload my field notebook, camera, binoculars, water bottle, and pencils from my old green field pack. I chuck the pack in the tent and transfer the other items to my scope pack, and then drape my binoculars around my neck. I leave camp and head for the rim, searching the sky for that familiar shape—a crossbow silhouetted against a bright blue sky. The vantage point I need has to be catty-cornered to the towering rock formation called Pico Cerdo. Walking is easy, as the top of the escarpment is made up of grassland interspersed with sotol and maguey plants.

I find a level spot with a rock that I can prop my back against. From this vantage point, I can see the towering cliff face perfectly. The scope only takes a minute to set up. I look northwest—the view is incredible. I am a giant, I can move the mountains like chess pieces. Let's see, I can move the Chisos eastward a little and they would be on Black Gap. I move Santiago Peak and Nine Point Mesa northeast a little. I can crown the queen with Elephant Mountain and the king will be Cathedral Peak. Incredible, the entire Big Bend is laid out before me.

A high thin creaking sound brings me back to reality. The sound gives me chills, and I feel the goosebumps pop up on my arms. I have heard this sound hundreds of times in the last seventeen years. Once you have heard it, you never forget it. A female peregrine is telling the world that she knows you are here. And she is not pleased! I turn the scope quickly. Squinting through the eyepiece I search the massive gray rock tower, checking each hole and overhang. Bingo! I hold my breath and then let it out slowly.

She is beautiful. Facing me, I see the dark hood on her head. The yellow cere is bright above the heavy dark beak. Her eyes can only be described as glaring. She is looking directly at me and her dark liquid eyes stare unblinkingly. She voices her displeasure again, the high thin sound carrying on the mountain air. Her mate will be here shortly. He heard her before I did. I grab my binoculars and search the sky. He surprises me. I hear the wind in his wings as his flight cuts the air like a hot knife in butter, a mini-jet. I drop the binoculars. He is above me flying fast and purposefully toward the cliff. The long pointed wings beat like synchronized oarsmen paddling a fast canoe. His underparts are startlingly white barred with black, his legs and huge feet are tucked up, their color like old dried corn. He turns, the sunlight glinting on his blue-black feathers. He is gorgeous. I sigh; I knew they had to be here. This is too perfect a place.

She is *la reina de la sierra* (the queen of the mountain), he is *el rey* (the king). They rule this wild Mexican mountain. I am an intruder, an interloper in their world. He flies by the eyrie on the cliff where *la reina* is incubating her clutch of blotchy brown and white eggs. Realizing that she is okay, he turns his attention back to me. He circles higher and higher gaining altitude until he is tiny black speck in the clear blue sky. I lose him in the vastness, but I know he sees every move I make.

I settle down for a wait, maybe short, maybe long. It is four o' clock. She will leave the eggs before dark to fly and stretch her wings and to feed from a cache he has stored for her, or she will make her own kill. He will incubate the eggs while she is out feeding and exercising. I watch and wait in silence. At five-thirty the shadows are lengthening, she rises off the eggs and ruffles her feathers. Slowly, ever so carefully, she picks up each foot, placing it softly ahead of her until she is away from her precious eggs. I grin. What a gait! She looks like a wounded crab as she scrabbles around and walks out on the ledge. She looks westward and vocalizes, a sound like a rusty hinge squeaking. She is calling for *el rey*, telling him that it is his turn, she needs to stretch.

I watch her closely, knowing she will see him before I do. That is the way of the peregrine. She tenses: he's coming in. She tells me this by her actions. She lifts off the cliff effortlessly and I hear his fast stoop, sounding for all the world like the roar of a jet. He is plunging downward, slashing the wind. It is his way—he is the silver bullet. He lifts his wings and turns, coming toward the cliff like a B-52 on a strafing run. He has the afterburners on and comes into the small hole in the cliff without slowing. Incredibly, the simple unfolding and uplifting of his long powerful wings turns his stoop flight into slow motion. He lands on the ledge in a single smooth movement. He scuttles inside the hole and I see him carefully step over the eggs. He settles down lightly, like a butterfly on a blossom, light as air itself and nothing short of amazing. I have watched this theatre thousands of times, yet it never ceases to amaze me. I watch him through the scope. The dark fierce eyes see all and fear nothing.

I pick up the binoculars and search for the female. She will exercise and feed for about an hour and then return to her precious eggs for the night. She is high in the sky; the sun is sinking in the west. She turns with a flick of her wings and stoops sharply. The setting sun turns her to rose-purple as she sinks out of sight below the rim. I make final field notes, do sketches of their head patterns, determine my precise location via the geographic positioning system (GPS), and wait for her return. *El rey* is asleep on the eggs. It is so quiet and still that the only audible sounds are myself breathing and the wind whispering softly through the sotol.

I check the time, 6:15 p.m., and then swing the scope to the eyrie. The king is looking north. He rises carefully and lifts each foot forward, setting each down in turn. Once he is away from the eggs, he too crab-walks to the edge of the hole. The king surveys his domain, and what a domain

he has. *La reina* comes in over my head in a whirl-wind flight. They move simultaneously; like dancers drifting apart, he lifts, she lands. She hurries to her eggs. She worries, as he is good, but she is better. She moves over the eggs, bending down to turn each of the eggs with her beak. The same heavy beak adapted for killing is gentle as a softly falling snowflake on this occasion. She turns carefully, placing each foot just so. She faces outward and settles down over her eggs. Her warm belly covers the dark eggs like a soft wool blanket. She is content but ever so watchful.

I break down the scope, finish my notes, and head to camp feeling rich. I wonder what the poor humans are doing today. I am grateful for wild peregrines and wild mountains to watch them from. I slip the pack from my shoulders and put it inside the tent. My radio crackles, the harsh sound violating the mountain silence. My husband asks, "How's it going?"

"Great," I reply, "I found them." We talk briefly and I check out. The wind is coming up out of the south. It smells balmy, a Gulf wind promising rain and tropical nights. At coffee time, I start a fire and boil coffee in my old blue enamel pot. My tin cup looks like it has survived many battles. I sip the brew and have dinner.

Darkness comes early to the mountain. I write in my daily journal by flashlight. I take the last cup of coffee and bank the glowing embers. I sit quietly sipping the coffee. Lights far to the north in Texas look like fireflies on a summer night.

South in Mexico it is an even black. No lights mar the vastness of northern Coahuila. A perfect day. I yawn—it is time for bed, yet I am reluctant to go inside. The night is beautiful, stars shine in a blue-black velvet sky. The breeze rustles the blades of the sotol plants and the dry seeds inside old lechuguilla blooms rattle like miniature rattlesnakes.

I rise and dump the coffee grounds on the fire and prepare the pot for coffee tomorrow morning. As I unzip the tent, I hear *la reina* softly wail. I stop and listen—the sound so high and thin on the night wind has an eerie quality. Perhaps she is telling me good night. I salute the queen, *buenas noches, reina, dulce sueño*. A thought comes to mind, one of my mentors telling me long ago, "Never anthropomorphize, it's a bad habit." I smile—what the hell, I'm on top of a Mexican mountain and if I want to think a falcon called goodnight, I can. Tomorrow will be different, back to business.

I climb in the sleeping bag, bright purple no less. I toss and turn trying to get comfortable. The tent crackles in the wind, and I feel as if I am caught in a potato chip bag. I curl up and listen to the night sounds, thankful that I am here. I think back to yet another peregrine falcon, a male who I had watched grow up. He always came in on strafing runs like a bomber when I entered his territory. I named him Pepe, and his mate, a big female, I named Rosita. They too were on a Mexican mountain, twelve hundred feet above the river on a sheer limestone cliff. I watched them for six years until they disappeared one spring. I also banded their daughter Sola, while they screamed their displeasure and made mock attacks at me. Well, not so mock, as I recall that Pepe knocked my cap off. I smile; they are awesome birds.

I am up early; dawn breaks and I am anticipating the hot coffee bubbling on the small fire. I head outside and make the coffee, pour a thermos full, and heft my pack onto my shoulders. I use the flashlight and walk carefully, not wanting to step on a rattlesnake. I set up at yesterday's observation point. *La reina* is ready for the new day. She wails softly, the sound caressing the crisp morning air. She is ready to stretch her wings and feed after tending the eggs all night. I wonder if she spent a sleepless night, apprehensive about the strange object in her world. I can't tell her that I am not a threat. My report will tell no one where she is, only Eyrie #004, Coahuila, Mexico. Her secret is safe with me. *El rey* comes in, looking black in the first light, and she leaves. I check the time. I have about two hours before the chopper arrives. I watch him on the eggs and then search for her. I make notes and check the time.

If I were here every day I would know their routine; they are creatures of habit, varying their daily patterns only occasionally. She rises from below me, and I draw a sharp breath, struck again by her beauty. She rides the wind like she owns it, the power exuded in every move of her wings is magnificent, mesmerizing. She turns and quickly flies to the cliff. I salute her, without a doubt *la reina de la sierra*.

The male, or tiercel, lifts off the ledge and meets her. She feints left, playing with the wind, and he follows. They caress the wind, drifting idly, and then she turns like a puppet on a wire, stooping into the wind, shining like a silver coin. Enough, she says, time for business. The long powerful legs drop like gear on an airplane. She lands ever so lightly and then enters the eyrie.

I rise and head back to camp to pack. My fire is dead; I shovel dirt on it and then pour the coffee dregs over that. I break camp quickly and lug the packs to the place where we landed yesterday. At 9:00 I hear the sounds of the helicopter blades: the chopper is on time.

I then hear the tiercel screeching his anger at the invader. I turn for one last look. The tiercel is riding the wind, twisting and turning in the morning sun. Suddenly he pulls his long wings back. Faster and faster he stoops, his body compressed, arrow-shaped as he plunges downward. I hear the falcon's high, thin wail.

The chopper comes in like an angry bee, shattering the spell. I stow my gear and climb aboard. We turn homeward and I turn to stare out the window at the mountain.

Many years ago when I saw my first peregrine falcon, I thought, "Well, now that I have seen them, I will not need to search for them anymore." I was wrong. On a day in April 2006, I was on the west side of El Jardín. Beto, Jonás, and I had hiked in to pick up a dropped telemetry collar and, on the way out of the twisting narrow canyon that marks the entrance, we spotted another pair of peregrines. They were about two miles from my observation point years ago. I stopped and watched them in courtship flight, I wondered if they could be the grandson or granddaughter of the pair I watched then on this same mountain.

I am still obsessed with their ways—the wild flights in raging winds, the figure eights and loop-de-loops in a clear blue sky, their fierce killing instinct, sometimes controlled, and sometimes an inimical frenzy. The dark liquid eyes, possessing a quality so fierce that it says to all, "I am the ruler," in the remote wild country they call home. No, once was not enough. There will never be enough peregrine days in hot winds, or starry nights on Mexican mountains when the high, wavering cry of a peregrine brings involuntary goosebumps to my skin. CEMEX El Carmen owns portions of both El Jardín and Cañón del Diablo, and these areas are wholly protected. This wild country with towering cliffs, deep canyons, and solitude are the perfect peregrine palaces. I hope they remain that way with as little disturbance as possible for time *ad infinitum*.

7 Campo Cinco, Pumas, and Spotted What's-Its

Campo Cinco is high in the Carmens, another meadow in the fir-pine forest. Formerly it was called Campo Madera, a lumber camp and hub of activity during the logging operation years. Several wood-plank houses, clotheslines, and tons of broken glass, plastic bottles, tires, and general junk littered the area. Once it was cleaned up, it looked like a different place. One small wooden hut remains in the clearing today. A huge pile of sawdust had us all shaking our heads about how to remove it. Every rainstorm caused the tannin from the sawdust to leach out into the small stream, coloring the water a rusty red.

Finally, the sawdust was mixed with the soil, and much of it was removed and hauled down the mountain to use as mulch. Today, native grasses and pine seedlings are growing in the area. It isn't a large area, but rather an opening in the forest of several acres with mountain muhly grass, southwestern chokecherry, wildflowers, and huge limestone boulders. Carmen Mountain white-tails graze peacefully here in the small meadow. Campo Cinco is a central point in the high country of the Carmens. From here you can turn upward to Campo Tres, Pico Loomis, Campo Dos, and Mesa Bonita. Drive eastward a little ways and head downward to Cañón Carboneras and Campo Uno. Two events occurred at Campo Cinco that I will always remember—one was very funny, and the other dramatic, in the life-and-death sense.

The life-and-death incident occurred several years ago. At the time, Jonás and I were headed up the mountain on four-wheelers to collect plants on the way to Campo Uno. Mauro Alonso, the mechanic for El Carmen, was about thirty minutes in front of us. He called on the radio and said that a puma had just killed a Carmen Mountain white-tail doe right in the road. We thanked him for the information and gunned the four-wheelers up the mountain. We reached Cinco and the doe was still warm and bleeding. With our disturbance, the puma had moved off into the forest, but I am sure that he was hidden nearby. We radioed Pilares and asked Billy Pat to bring us a remote camera on his way up the mountain. While we waited for him to arrive, we hid in the firs and boulders and watched for the puma, but there was no sign of it. I am sure the cat was watching us look for it.

About an hour and a half later, Billy Pat arrived and we hauled the doe up the hill, wired her to a tree, and then set two remote cameras. We knew the puma would be back. We quickly left the area and headed down to Campo Uno to collect plants. On the way down the canyon, I was thinking about the peacefulness of that small meadow with deer grazing, the small creek trickling, and the firs whispering in the wind. I could imagine the puma lying motionless, waiting with infinite patience for the right moment to jump on the doe. Perhaps the wind was perfect and in his favor; the deer probably never sensed his presence and the attack was swift and typical, a quick rush breaking her neck. While she lay bleeding and kicking, her lifeblood was draining away, and the puma anticipated his meal. Perhaps he had not eaten in several days, or maybe it was a female with cubs to feed. Life and death in nature are daily occurrences. Hopefully, it balances out and enough creatures are born and survive so that others may also survive. Predators and prey are never pretty stories, but they do summarize reality for many species.

Pumas are large solitary cats that have very extensive home ranges. They prefer fresh meat

Campo Cinco, 2002

over tainted and often go several days without food. They are high-class predators, but even they miss their marks at times. The puma's favorite prey in northern Mexico and western Texas is deer, and if they are not available, other species such as javelina, cottontail, black-tailed jackrabbits, porcupines, and other small mammals, and even turkeys, are fair game. Desert bighorn sheep populations suffer heavily from puma depredations. The puma has also been hunted with dogs and trapped for many years in efforts to combat depredations on the native bighorns that have been reintroduced in the southwestern United States. Pumas will also kill domestic livestock, particularly sheep and goats. At present the puma is still fairly common in western Texas and northern Coahuila, perhaps because of their penchant for high rim-rock country and inaccessible terrain, particularly in the desert country.

We finished our fieldwork for the day and headed back toward Cinco. The deer had not been disturbed, but we knew the puma would return after dusk. The next morning we headed back up the mountain, and checking the carcass and camera was foremost on our minds. We reached Cinco and the camera was out of film, and the carcass had been wrestled around and fed upon. Hopeful that we had the images on film, we changed rolls and headed out to work. About a month later I got the slides back and found that we did get photos of the puma. Judging from its size, the cat appeared to be a female. She was definitely not hap-py that her fresh kill had somehow gotten caught in a tree. After wrestling with the carcass quite a bit, she finally decided to dine right there.

The second event that I remember vividly at Campo Cinco was in July 2003. Feliciano, Jonás, and I had been at Campo Dos for five days netting bats and sampling small mammals. We decided to move to Campo Cinco on the last day and put out mist nets across the small creek. We loaded the truck and headed down the mountain in late afternoon. We quickly set up the nets, built a small campfire and cooked dinner, and then had a cup of Feliciano's famous *café con leche* (coffee with milk). Darkness was approaching and I was hoping for a good night of bat netting. We took turns walking down and checking the nets; it was cold for July, and we were bundled up in jackets while sitting near our small campfire. The night stretched on. No bats in the nets. We chatted, had more coffee, and talked some more. No action in the nets, and it was getting colder, so we all grabbed blankets from the truck and wrapped up. Jonás took his blanket and headed to the small side porch at the old camp house. Feliciano and I stayed bundled up in chairs closer to the fire.

I dozed off, and then woke up and walked down to check the nets at 5:30 a.m. The wind was up and the nets were empty. I hurried back up the hill to the warmth of the campfire. I settled back in my blanket and had just dozed off again when Feliciano starts yelling "Spotted! Spotted! Spotted!" I jumped up and Jonás came running from the porch. Feliciano was jumping around the camp chairs and the fire while still hollering "Spotted!" The first thing I thought of was spotted bats. I'd been hoping to catch spotted bats in the Carmens. After years of netting at the Black Gap and not catching this species I thought I would surely find them here.

I started looking skyward in the predawn light, expecting to see them flying, but I saw absolutely nothing. Feliciano was still hopping around and muttering about spotted things and poking a stick at something on the ground. It was still too dark to see much of anything. I couldn't imagine spotted bats on the ground, but by his gyrations and mutterings it seemed that the spotted whatever was on the ground. I peered over the back of the chair toward a small pile of rocks that Feliciano was now aiming for and saw a spotted skunk. That poor skunk was running around with Feliciano in hot pursuit, and the absence of spraying was truly a miracle. We laughed until our sides hurt. We didn't catch the skunk, and we sure didn't get spotted bats like I had hoped. Actually, the spotted skunk was important, as we had not yet documented this species in the Carmens since we had commenced the baseline inventory. This species was previously documented by Ernest Marsh in 1936 when he reported seeing a dead spotted skunk in El Jardín, and then Rollin Baker collected a specimen south of Boquillas in the 1950s. We didn't get a photo, but later in the summer another spotted skunk encounter occurred that I didn't think was funny.

Santiago was at Campo Uno monitoring elk telemetry and decided to spend the night since it was late afternoon and he had a long drive back down the mountain to headquarters. As the story goes, early the next morning the camp cook discovered a skunk under a chair and immediately vacated the premises and called Santi. The cook believed that since Santi was a wildlife biology person, then he should be the one to remove the skunk. We had a large camp set up there at the time with men cleaning up and building a large log cabin, and the cook was a busy man with no time for skunks in the kitchen.

Santi sauntered into the cookhouse and somehow managed to grab the spotted skunk without getting sprayed. He then looked around and decided that he could put the skunk in an ice chest, a new medium-sized one. He proceeded to do just that, and then placed the ice chest on his four-wheeler and fastened it in place with bungee cords. Santiago then had breakfast, loaded his gear, and started the drive from Campo Uno to Los Pilares headquarters, a drive of no less than two hours. He called us on the radio to say that he had a live spotted skunk; no details followed. We could only wonder at the time how he was progressing down the mountain with a live skunk. Shortly Santi roared into Pilares on the four-wheeler with the shiny new blue ice chest tied on the back. We proceeded to figure out a way to get the skunk out of the ice chest without being sprayed. Jonás opened the lid slowly, and the skunk still hadn't sprayed. I imagined that the skunk was probably in shock and disoriented after his wild ride down the mountain. Jonás grabbed the skunk by the scruff of the neck, and we got ready to photograph him. Jonás turned toward me, holding the skunk away from his body, and the skunk immediately raised his tail and sprayed me full in the face. After I managed to get my breath, which wasn't easy, I wiped my eyes and finished coughing and gasping. The only option, I decided, was to drive home, around twelve miles distant, and take a bath in tomato juice. When I returned to Pilares later that day, we had our first record of the spotted skunk for the Carmens.

The spotted skunk is distributed in the Carmens from the mid elevations to the higher pine-oak-fir forest. This small skunk prefers habitats with many rocky outcrops, ledges with overhangs, and areas with many cavities in rocks. One individual may have only a few spots and be predominantly black, whereas the next individual may be heavily marked with spots. The local name for the species is *zorillo moteado*. Perhaps since Baker and Marsh conducted fieldwork in the area, this species has become more common and extended its range upward into the higher pine-oak forests.

Late one night returning from Múzquiz, I was driving up Cañón el Álamo (also called San Isidro) to our house. It was about 2:00 a.m., and I was fighting sleep and thinking that the road got longer with every trip I made late at night. I rounded the last curve right below our house and slammed on the brakes. Walking down the middle of the road was a female spotted skunk with three tiny young. All had their tails raised marching in single file and were apparently unconcerned that a monster truck was right behind them. I patiently waited until they exited the road into the arroyo. I had learned my lesson about spotted skunks and had no desire to renew the acquaintance up close.

Cuadra Pelota translates to a playing field for a ball game, according to locals in the Carmens. The area is one of the most scenic in the mountains. The road winds downward to a meadow of grasses with towering cliffs of volcanic rock called "tuff." On the north side are numerous caves and holes, and a thick forest of pine, fir, and oak is found on the steep hill at the south side. This area is always peaceful and a small group of Carmen Mountain white-tailed deer can normally be seen here on an everyday basis. At the base of the meadow, wildlife avail themselves of water in a small arroyo with a seep. Mexican jays, black-crested titmice, yellow-eyed juncos, and acorn woodpeckers are the most common birds in the area and are permanent residents. I have also seen many black bear in this area.

The old fallen logs and debris on the forest floor above the meadow are home to a small mammal that the area is famous for. Miller's shrew was first collected in the Carmens by F. W. Miller in 1940 (Baker 1956). Little information is available on the life history of this species in northern Coahuila. In October 2003, we were conducting small mammal surveys in this area and much to our surprise we found a nest of Miller's shrews in the meadow at Cuadra Pelota. The nest was located under a decaying tree trunk at the entrance of a Botta's pocket gopher tunnel. The small, loosely constructed cup of grass blades and pine needles had a side opening and the top fitted flush against the bot-

Miller's shrew. Photo J.D. Villalobos, 2003

tom of the decaying log. The adult fled into the Botta's pocket gopher tunnel, leaving the six young in the nest. The adult was a brownish gray color with an elongated nose. The six young all had their eyes closed and their elongated noses were a fleshy pink. Their pelage was very short and a soft chocolate brown color, and their tails were hairless. We retained two for voucher specimens and returned the rest to the nest. This was the first documented nesting of Miller's shrews in the Carmens (Delgadillo et al. 2005).

Once we had found the first nest, we began to find others in similar habitats and elevations in the high mountain country. During the course of our baseline inventory, we documented two species of shrews in the Carmens. The desert shrew inhabits the lower desert elevations to the higher grassland of sotol, beaked yucca, and scattered junipers, and the Miller's shrew inhabits meadows in the mixed-conifer mesic montane forest up to over 2,700 meters.

We have yet to study this small shrew to document more of its life history, such as diet, whether they hibernate in the winter when the winds howl and layers of ice cover the ground, and the number of young in the average litter, among many other topics. Perhaps we will study this tiny mammal in coming years to determine its life history, or perhaps we will just check on them occasionally to be sure that they are still here and doing well. As long as the habitat is protected, humans do not intrude, and the mountain haven remains intact, the Miller's shrew should have a bright future.

Meadow at Cuadra Pelota, 2003

9 La Laguna

I had heard of La Laguna in the Carmens many years ago. While flying telemetry on radio-collared black bears that had crossed the border from Texas to Mexico, I studied it many times from the plane. Taking the road east from Campo Uno, you travel a couple of kilometers on a rocky road going up a little in elevation, where the forest opens to a park-like setting of pine-oak woodland. Abruptly you round a curve and catch your first glimpse of the laguna, a shallow natural lake on top of a mountain. How it was formed we may never know, and the soil is different from the surrounding area. Just a few feet from the water's edge the soil is red clay, yet in the laguna the soil is almost like bentonite, but not quite. There are no drainages running into the laguna, and it is dependent on rains to fill the basin. It is not a huge laguna, being roughly three hundred meters in length and about the same in width. Rocks jut out of the water, and in the center it is about a meter deep. The clay-type soil holds water year-round unless it is unusually dry. There are no fish in any of the mountain streams or in the laguna. But the laguna has snails, fairy shrimp, and water bugs of all sorts, and the grasses and horsetails and sedges that grow in the shallows provide a lush smorgasbord for the Carmen Mountain white-tailed deer, black bear, wintering ducks, and shorebirds; the laguna is also a source of water for all wildlife in this area. Pico Mabrico stands guard on the east end and the laguna is surrounded on all sides by the pine-oak woodland. The view is breathtaking, especially in summer after the rains when the area is lush, wildflowers are plentiful, and to the north a high mountain waterfall can be seen.

In the fall months, especially September and October, migrating shorebirds, ducks, and later in the season, geese, all find food and shelter in this haven. It is not uncommon in winter to observe Mexican X mallards (hybrids of Mexican ducks and mallards), mallards, ring-necked ducks, green-winged and cinnamon teal, northern pintails, American wigeon, northern shoveler, killdeer, great blue herons, and a host of songbirds. Mexican X mallards and killdeer nest here.

La Laguna, 2003

One September day in 2003, we counted twenty-six willets—they were literally asleep on their feet resting during a stopover on their fall migration. We were able to observe them at very close range. This was a new bird record for the Carmens. Willets had not previously been recorded here and we haven't observed them since. They are easy to identify with their plump bodies and distinct black and white under-wing pattern. I will always remember the sight of all twenty-six lined up like bowling pins on the rock outcroppings. One would move, another would move into his place, and the line would reform. We watched this particular behavior for over an hour. I had no clue what this shifting and moving meant, but it was well choreographed. The next day they had headed south, perhaps to the Mexican coast or even farther.

White-throated swifts are resident species in the Carmens and they can be seen daily soaring and darting over the laguna in their missile-like flights. Two other resident species that use the laguna on a regular basis for their hunting grounds are the Cooper's hawk and peregrine falcon. Watching a peregrine dive at speeds close to two hundred miles an hour, grab a lunch of green-winged teal in its talons, and head for a nearby perch—all in a single motion—is always a remarkable experience. Cooper's hawks hunt the open areas but are also at home darting through the pine oak woodlands in search of a songbird.

Butterflies also frequent the muddy areas

along the edges of the laguna, taking nectar from the many wildflowers there. Common species are pipevine swallowtails, American and painted ladies, monarchs, Mexican silverspots, variegated fritillary, sleepy orange, and a host of others. One special butterfly we have found near the laguna is the sandia hairstreak (*Callophrys mcfarlandi*), which prefers bear grass, according to my friend and butterfly expert Jim Brock.

La Laguna is also a mecca for wildflowers, including one of the most beautiful plants in the Carmens, the cinnabar ladies' tresses, which can be found here on occasion. The plant is tall and slender with a heavy bloom, an orchid with a flame orange flower. The leaves are about one and a half inches wide and ten to twelve inches long and medium green in color. I don't see it every year, and it isn't abundant, but it is always a glorious surprise when it blooms after the late summer rains in September. This species is limited in distribution, found in small numbers here in the Carmens, the adjacent Coahuila mountains, and western Texas in several locations.

A peaceful setting, this laguna on top of a mountain has probably been here for thousands of years. On hot summer days when we are working in the high country, there is nothing I would rather do than head to La Laguna, relax in the shade of a pine tree, and watch wildlife, butterflies, and birds during my lunch hour. The Carmen Mountain white-tailed deer are calm, only glancing at uninvited guests as they are busy wading out belly deep in the warm water, pulling mouthfuls of lush grasses and sedges. A peregrine falcon soars overhead, checking out dinner prospects. Killdeer call and frogs jump from the muddy edges into the water when disturbed. A black hawk circles—she too is looking for lunch, and a frog or a snake will do. Puffy clouds build to the north in Texas like popcorn balls, and the wind softly rustles the pine needles. All seems in perfect harmony here, nature at her finest high on the mountain.

Claret cup cactus, La Laguna, 2003

10 Cañón el Oso

Starting high in the Carmens above Campo Dos, and continuing even higher toward Campo Tres where these canyons fork, is the beginning of Cañón el Oso, so named for the many black bears that inhabit this area. It is a long winding canyon of consummate scenic beauty. Starting at Campo Dos and hiking down to Campo Uno is a hike that should not be hurried, but one to be enjoyed every step of the way. I have found something different to stop and photograph or collect on every trip I have made down this canyon. Even on the hottest summer day, the canyon provides respite from the heat under a canopy of oak, fir, and pine. There is a mountain stream with hundreds of mini-waterfalls that rush downward to Camp Uno, filling the lake with water, and then spilling over the dam downward into Cañón de Botella. Eventually the water reaches El Club on the east side and the desert grasslands at Ejido Morelos.

I have hiked this canyon in all seasons of the year. Once in December, with about three inches of snow on the ground, Feliciano, Jonás, and I hiked part way down accompanied by three Mexican biologists from Zacatecas. It was bitter cold and windy, but the canyon was a winter wonderland. Everything was covered in white, pine and fir branches bent downward, laden with snow—it was very quiet, and no birds were singing, not even the ever-present Mexican jays. The day was cloudy and dark and the canyon even darker, but beautiful. The rocks in the creek all had their tops covered with pristine snow; the only tracks were ours.

Another day, Feliciano, Jonás, and I hiked downward to Campo Uno collecting plants, when we were caught in a thunderstorm and sought cover under a huge Coahuila fir. It provided shelter from the storm, which spent itself after a few minutes, and we were once again immersed in sunshine.

Cañón el Oso, 2004

Cañón el Oso is a lesson in plant diversity and elevation—you only have to stroll along and look around to note the changes in vegetation as you descend. Starting at Campo Dos, the trail drops off from the road and winds down to a small open area that is predominantly pine and fir. You enter this segment of the trail at the highest point, and then start the gradual descent to Campo Uno. Following the creek and crossing it in many places, you see the remains of the old road that connected Campo Tres down through this canyon to the sawmill at Campo Uno. It is amazing that a vehicle driver would even attempt to negotiate the top part of the canyon.

The trail follows the creek, and the old road is a series of rocky ledges that spiral downward to the creek bottom, leveling out for a short distance, then climbing, and then sloping gently downward again. This pattern continues all the way down the length of the canyon. Coming around a curve in the trail you see the remains of a bridge. Huge timbers were cut and braced across the creek. Flash flooding took the bridge many years ago. Towering overhead are the sheer cliffs of Cañón Escondido on the east side. Pines cling precariously to the cliff face, and ferns, agaves, and wildflowers dot the lower slopes of the cliff. Continuing downward you follow the creek on a narrow trail, crossing in several places on moss-covered rocks, climbing over deadfalls, and all the way you can't help but notice bear sign. For many years bears have used this canyon as a travel route. Trees bear the marks of their claws and bite marks, and the trail is littered with old and new scat.

In the thick canopy along the trail, you catch glimpses of a bigger patch of blue sky and towering cliffs. Basswood trees are abundant along with flowering dogwood and a host of other shrubs and trees. Farther along you catch a glimpse of blue sky and cliffs on the southwest side of the canyon. Abruptly you round a bend in the trail and hear yet another stream rushing downward. This is drainage from the Campo Cinco area. High above in the Cinco, this creek is only a small meandering brook, but once it enters the canyons below, it gains momentum, hurtling downward over huge boulders, waterfalls, and dead tree trunks, and is joined by smaller tributaries from numerous springs. When it reaches the canyon bottom, it rushes into the Cañón el Oso drainage and adds a tremendous amount of water to the already rushing creek. Never have I seen such beautiful mini-waterfalls and swirling pools, some deep enough to swim in, all bordered by lush vegetation and wildflowers in spring and summer.

Still farther down canyon, you see the jutting rock formation known as *El Divisadero* (The Divide), which towers above Cañón el Oso, also on the southwest side. This area is only a short distance from Campo Cinco on the road to Campo Uno. You make a left turn and meander toward the east a couple of kilometers and then walk out on a rocky point. The view is striking—below is Cañón el Oso; farther down the canyon at Campo Uno, the *presa* (small lake with a dam) is glimmering in the sun; in the near distance on the desert is Ejido Morelos; and directly north are the cliffs of Maravillas Canyon on the Black Gap Wildlife Management Area in West Texas.

Fir-pine forest in Cañón el Oso, 2004

Returning to the hike down the canyon, the terrain opens up suddenly into a park-like grassy area with oaks and ponderosa pine. The canyon opens even wider and you walk along the old logging road that leads directly to Campo Uno. Here the pools are wider and deep, where the water slows, filling the deep pools and then spilling downward to the next one. As you walk alongside the creek bank, leopard frogs jump into the water making a flat-sounding plop when they land—apparently they have never gone beyond the belly flop stage. Butterflies dance across the pools, and multi-hued dragonflies, including red, orange, blue, and a stunning black-and-white variety, dance over the water. Grasses are more abundant, where muhlys and gramas dominate. We see Carmen Mountain white-tails that gaze at us wide-eyed as we stop to take photos. Wild mushrooms of every shape and color grow in the humus below the trees. One of the most outstanding is the boletus species.

Montezuma quail are abundant in this area.

Montezuma quail in Cañón el Oso, 2004

Once we almost stepped on a male, who was hovering over four small chicks. The hen had hurried off with another two chicks. We watched him cover the chicks with his feathers, remaining perfectly still. His harlequin face markings and mottle brown plumage blended in with the forest floor cover. We backed off and left him to his parental duties.

A little farther down the canyon is the site of an old logging and vaquero camp. All that remains are parts of the corral and a cable stretching upward into the canyon. Perhaps they moved logs from the higher country via the cable down this canyon.

One day in June 2004, Billy Pat had dropped off Jonás and me at the Campo Dos trailhead with plans to collect us a couple of hours later at Campo Uno. We hiked down the trail collecting plants. Just as we crossed the last creek, we heard the unmistakable call of a common black hawk. We had observed a pair here earlier in the spring and figured they were nesting nearby. We stopped and listened and suddenly saw both the male and female circling nearby. We backed into the cover of a large rock outcrop that was covered by overhanging tree limbs and quietly waited for the adults to settle down—perhaps the female would go back to the nest. Shortly we saw her land in a nearby ponderosa and then take off and fly to another ponderosa. Sure enough, the nest was sequestered in a fork of two dead branches. Two chicks were in the nest calling for food. From my previous work with common black hawks in West Texas, I judged the young to be a little over twenty days old. We got photos of both adults. Two years later, we photographed another juvenal near the same location. Common black hawks are easy to spot in the Carmens, as several pair nest in the higher mountains as well as lower in the riparian areas of Juárez and Moreno Canyons. Common black hawks prefer riparian habitats with shallow pools of moving water. Their diet consists mainly of frogs, snakes, and other reptiles and amphibians. They are migratory, leaving in September and returning in mid to late March.

Soon the trail widens slightly and you walk into Camp Uno at the end of Cañón el Oso. This canyon, one of the most diverse and pristine in the Carmens, remains undisturbed, a haven for plants and wildlife.

Drought in the Chihuahuan Desert country is a dreaded event. We had been extremely lucky in the Carmens for several years, whereas our neighbors in West Texas and Chihuahua and other areas of Coahuila had suffered greatly because of prolonged drought. We were accustomed to rushing creeks, a desert blooming in spring that awed photographers, cool moist canyons in the high country, green grasses, abundant fruits and nuts for wildlife, and getting caught in nearly daily in summer showers. The location and elevation of the Carmens literally capture all the Gulf moisture that heads up from the south. The clouds build and then hang over the high mountain peaks, bringing rain to the sierra as well as downward and out to the desert flats. The Carmens are selfish, keeping the moisture until it is all used up.

Spring came early in 2005, and there had been little winter moisture. Grasses greened early, and then came the winds, first howling out of the north, and then changing direction and blowing daily from the west. Roads turned to powdered dust, grasses turned brown, and flowers tried in vain to bloom. Drought was even more evident in the high country. Mushrooms and orchids didn't push upward from the soil, and the forest smelled like hot pine. We watched the sky: little rain fell, just a shower here and one there. Creek levels began dropping and pools were shrinking.

We endured the long hot summer, but wildlife still looked

good and an occasional shower rushed across the mountain face or down below in the desert. Fall approached—there was no blaze of fall color in the sierra, leaves stayed on the trees, and creeks were nearly dry. We watched clouds, listened to weather reports, and hoped for rain. Nothing significant fell, only *chipe*, *chipe*, as the locals call a brief shower. There were no foggy mornings when clouds were low on the desert and the mountain shrouded. Winter came fast on the calendar but the weather remained mild. Wind and more wind from every direction and no rain. Christmas came and went, and the New Year roared in on a north wind. February and March 2006 were unseasonably warm, t-shirt days with a light jacket early in the morning. We were monitoring wildlife daily. They still looked remarkably healthy given the drought conditions. In April, hot

Forest fire at Mesa Escondido, 2006

sweltering heat with no respite, and more wind; desert plants were shrinking, dropping their leaves to conserve moisture. The prickly pears turned a deathly shade of pale yellow, and even the purple prickly pear did not turn green again in the spring and summer of 2006. The desert didn't bloom—the parched landscape waited for rain.

Fire season was here, and clouds built and dissipated quickly in the hot winds, but still no rain. On May 2, 2006, clouds piled up—thunder rumbled across the darkening sky and lightning struck, but no rain fell. Mesa Escondido near Campo Tres in the high country was on fire. For days, crews tried to suppress the fire, and helicopters came in and dropped water. There were also fires nearby in the Serranías del Burro, the Sierra Encantada, and close to Saltillo, in the high sierras. Finally, the Mesa Escondido fire was suppressed, the major hot spots were out, and the crews headed out some fourteen days after the fire started.

Hot daytime temperatures, wind, and no rain followed, and the forest fire smoldered and then sprang back to life. Once again the Mesa Escondido was burning. However, this wasn't a bad fire as fires go. A few trees were lost mainly because the forest floor was burning. Years of accumulated leaf litter on the forest floor fueled the smoldering embers, then a log rolled, and another fire would start. This continued for thirty-two days. Finally, after a light rain when the fire burned into a rock scree, it was out. The charred forest floor

was a grim reminder of how fragile this ecosystem really is. From the logging operations of yesteryear, a colossal quantity of cut timber still remains on the forest floor. Add to this the normal leaf litter that falls each year. All it would take was another lightning strike to start a major fire.

June 2006 was hot and hotter, with daytime temperatures soaring above the hundred-degree mark, which was very unusual for this country. The ever-present wind continued blowing from all directions. Normally, when the low desert country heated up, we would move our field operations to the high country. This year there was no difference, as the mountain was baking too. Bears and other wildlife were very visible, moving to sources of water. Flowers didn't bloom and butterflies were sparse. The trees in the higher elevations did not put forth spring leaves, and the evergreen species were dropping leaves and needles.

On June 23, Billy Pat left early with plans to stop in Del Rio, Texas, and then to continue on to the Adams Ranch the next day. He called on the radio and said that clouds were building all the way to Del Rio. I told him we had mountains of clouds building also. Jonás and I headed to the bighorn sheep reserve to check water troughs and put out salt. We commented on the clouds, hoping that they would keep building and bring rain. The sky darkened, thunder rolled, and lightning zig-zagged across the black sky. Just as we reached Los Pilares, the skies opened, rain pelted down, and wonder of wonders we couldn't see the mountain for the heavy rain. Maybe this was the drought breaker. We checked the rain gauge at Los Pilares: one and a half inches, what a help that would be. Shortly we were back in the field checking where it rained. I called Campo Uno on the radio, but they reported only two-tenths of an inch. We hoped that the west face of the mountain received more. The low country was drenched, the pungent odor of creosote bush permeating the air. Arroyos were running and the tanks filling—what a relief. The rain came from the south across the west end of the Sierra Encantada and then spent itself on the west face of the Carmens. Only those areas in the path of the storm received the life-giving rain, but it was a start.

The drought continued. The land was parched, desert plants shrinking to conserve moisture within. High in the sierra, the oaks still lacked leaves. Walking the forest floor, the vegetation literally crumbled underfoot. The areas that received rain greened up in two days, a sharp contrast to the surrounding areas that didn't receive rain. People say that drought is cyclic. I hoped the cycle would break soon. I missed the rushing creeks, waterfalls shining like rivers of diamonds cascading down the cliffs. Orchids, wildflowers, oaks loaded with acorns, moist mountain canyons, and a lush desert full of blooms. Meantime, while we waited for these conditions to return, we dealt with the drought as best we could and

hoped for rain. My friend David Riskind assured me that he had seen the Carmens drier than this. I hope I never do.

In mid-August 2006, the rains came, enough to drench the mountains and low country. From that time through early September, rains fell nearly every day. This was more like it! We still needed more rain to replenish the springs, fill the tanks, and soak into the ground. Conditions were good again, and we heaved sighs of relief. The rains we received were life-savers to the plants and wildlife. We needed more, fall was coming early, and already the mornings were crisp. Did we dare hope for fall moisture?

Rains in lower desert, 2006

12 Los Pilares and Desert Bighorn Sheep

The desert bighorn ewe stood silhouetted against a blue sky high on the rim rock inside the entrance to Cañón el Álamo. She was soaking up the last warming rays of the evening sun, her face nearly all white, revealing her age. Nearby her lamb of the year lay sprawled on a limestone rock, also enjoying the sun. I watched her through my binoculars. She was staring directly west, motionless. I wondered if she was thinking of her homeland, the Isla del Tiburón in Sonora State. Her homeland in the Sonoran Desert, which blended directly into the Sea of Cortez, was a far cry from the Chihuahuan Desert that she now called home. Did she miss the cardón cactus, the blazing Sonoran sunsets, seeing whales in the sea, or never having seen or smelled a puma? Or was she content here?

This ewe, along with other sheep, made a long journey from the Sea of Cortez to Coahuila. First, they were net-gunned from a helicopter, carried on a boat to the mainland, and transported by trailer to the Yaqui Reserve. (The Reserve, created by CEMEX for the desert bighorn conservation program, is located near Hermosillo, Sonora, Mexico.) Several years later, she and others were recaptured by net gun, worked up and radio collared, and then transported some eighteen hundred miles to the Chihuahuan Desert in Coahuila. This is a stressful procedure for any wildlife, to say the least, but necessary if she were to be remembered as one of the founding members of the first wild herd of desert bighorns to roam these mountains in over fifty years.

Did she know how important she was? I doubted it. She couldn't have known that, when I went to bed at night, I hoped that she and the other members of the wild herd were safe on a Coahuila mountain, and that a puma was not padding along keeping a watchful eye, waiting on the perfect moment to make a kill.

The desert bighorn formerly roamed these desert mountains, but just like in western Texas, they were extirpated some fifty years ago. Rollin Baker sent me a photo of a desert bighorn taken by hunters in the late 1940s or 1950s in the Sierra de San Lázaro in Coahuila. This may have been the last recorded desert bighorn in the state. The desert bighorn in Coahuila was unevenly distributed in several desert mountain ranges and, like the Texas bighorn, also fell victim to diseases transmitted by domestic livestock, particularly sheep and goats; loss of habitat; and unregulated hunting.

The Texas Parks and Wildlife Department began a desert bighorn restoration program many years ago, and later the Texas Bighorn Society joined in helping put sheep back in West Texas. Today the state of Texas boasts more than one thousand desert bighorns scattered in seven different mountain ranges. During my tenure of almost ten years with the Department as a wildlife technician working at Black Gap, I learned a lot about desert bighorn ecology and what could go wrong in reintroductions. Desert bighorns are one of the toughest yet most fragile wildlife species I have worked with in my career. I have always thought of desert bighorn as chickens one day and feathers the next. A healthy herd might be doing well, lulling you into a false sense of security, when, seemingly overnight, right before your eyes, the sheep succumb to diseases picked up from something as small as a gnat, or are reduced to piles of bones by a female puma with two hungry yearlings. On one such occasion, I recall being tossed around in a Cessna 206 high above desert cliffs, listening to not one but several mortality signals on my radio transmitter.

Reintroducing desert bighorns is never easy—it takes years, money, politics, more money, surplus sheep, habitat, grueling days in desert heat, more money, heartbreak, more money, and years of all this, and maybe you have a successful bighorn sheep reintroduction. Yes, more money is still needed. But, you never really get comfortable because you know in the back of your mind that tomorrow everything can change.

The CEMEX El Carmen Project has an important mission and a challenge to restore lands and native wildlife to the Carmen Mountains. At the inception of this project in 2000, a top priority was the reintroduction of desert bighorn sheep to historic habitat in the Carmen Mountains. Help was enlisted from sheep biologists in Texas, New Mexico, and Mexico. The Los Pilares Criadero (brood facility) is an area of roughly 5,000 hectares (11,000 acres) enclosed in a high, predator-proof fence. Inside the fence, the area is typical

Chihuahuan Desert habitat and very conducive to bighorn sheep reproduction. The *criadero* encompasses a series of ridges that run in a north–south direction, comprised of igneous rock with ample boulder piles and caves for lambing and shade. About thirty-five kilometers of pipeline puts water on top of the ridges in a series of drinkers designed specifically for desert bighorns. The vegetation is Chihuahuan Desert shrub type, but also structurally similar to vegetation in Sonora. Once the fence was completed, Billy Pat and I traveled to the Carmens on a vacation and live-trapped and relocated black bears and puma that were inside the criadero. The gates were then shut, awaiting bighorns from Sonora.

In November 2000, one ram and two ewes were released inside the criadero; subsequently one ewe produced one lamb in 2001. We moved to Coahuila as managers of the El Carmen Project in October 2001, and shortly thereafter an additional forty-seven desert bighorns from Sonora were released inside the criadero. The criadero is so large that the desert bighorns literally do not know they are fenced in. Desert bighorns do not move around at great distance as long as they have adequate food sources, water, and good habitat. Habitat conditions here in Coahuila were actually better than in Sonora, and they were in a predator-free environment, a major factor in lamb production and survival. The desert bighorns have done extremely well, and the herd is growing with normal mortality.

The bighorns formed several groups, which have been named: the Tapón group, the Mazón group, the Sotolar Group, and the Lomas Prietas group. They are monitored several days every week and daily during the lambing season. The fence is checked practically every day, and water stations are checked in the lower elevations and on the high ridges. This herd of desert bighorns constitutes the brood stock for future releases in the Carmens, and in time for other areas of historic habitat.

This program represents an incredible investment of time, money, work, and commitment by CEMEX to return this native species to historic range. Is it worth it? Yes: the desert bighorn is one of the most majestic native desert species found in North America, but at the same time one of the most challenging. Of course, the recognition and glamour of returning this species to historic habitat are nice, but for me the most rewarding aspect is to see a desert bighorn high atop a rocky ridge, sky-lined like a carved monument—this is their home, their place in the natural world.

Several years ago after a long hot day of looking for new lambs, squinting through a spotting scope for hours on end with sweat running down in my eyes clouding my vision, wishing for a cold drink, and wondering which lamb belonged to which ewe, the sun finally sank behind the distant mountains in Chihuahua. Jonás and I finished comparing notes, drank a cold cup of coffee, and headed to the truck as dark approached. The

Desert bighorns at Los Pilares Criadero.
Photo J. D. Villalobos, 2004

sheep were on the tops of the ridges, bedding down for the night. We had counted twenty-four new lambs in a couple of days. Watching lambs running and jumping like so many popcorn balls, tumbling over rocks, skidding to stops and digging with their tiny hooves (imitating the adults), bedding down for siestas beside a big ram, and bleating to mama to wait because it was time for lunch is one of the most satisfying aspects of field work. Yes, we were tired, red-eyed, and ready to head in. We loaded the equipment into the truck and just a few feet away a great-horned owl landed on top of the fence and began calling.

Another answered from farther away. I turned to get in the truck and said, "Look, see the lights." Far away in Big Bend National Park we could see headlights like tiny pinpoints heading up the winding road to the Chisos Basin; closer but not much, we saw another set of headlights coming toward Rio Grande Village in the park. Here in Coahuila the inky blackness was not marred by a single light, the sheep were on the mountain, and we could call it a day.

It had been a special day because we had been treated to a bighorn show by the new lambs. Other days with bighorns here in Coahuila have been memorable, such as the day when we were hiking back in a canyon and we heard rocks falling and looked up; a ewe was headed our way, her black tongue hanging out, and directly behind her was a very determined ram with one thing on his mind. She had other ideas. We stopped and stared open-mouthed in amazement as they ran right by us. Another time we watched a young three-year-old ram work a ewe like a cutting horse works a calf. Every move she made, he blocked her attempt to go back to the top of the mountain. We watched him for over an hour—he was determined she was not getting away. Meanwhile, there was a big ram standing like a sentinel on the rim rock, but the young ram had decided this ewe was his. Another time during breeding season I watched a big ram on a rim full of boulders. He was focused on other ridges looking for rams.

Disappointed when he did not see any to challenge, he transferred his attention to a nearby boulder, lowered his head, and hit the rock full charge with his horns. Talk about misguided!

Lambing season is my favorite time. The ewes separate and find themselves secluded spots to give birth. Often they will stand for hours in one spot in the warm sunshine. We start looking for lambs as early as February. Sometimes it is easy, because we will see them near the ewe or nursing; tiny bighorns can move exceptionally well in a matter of hours. Other times we watch patiently through a spotting scope for hours, and finally see a tiny ear protruding from behind a bush.

One cold March morning when lambing season was in full swing, Jonás and I were in the criadero checking the bighorns. The wind was out of the north and cold. Clouds were scudding in over the peaks and rapidly covering the high mountain peaks, and then moving downward until they appeared to be rushing out onto the desert. Shortly the peaks in the criadero were covered. We were worried about the cold front. Cold rain or sleet and newborn lambs are not a good combination. We were gazing at clouds as they swirled around us, and visibility was next to zero. We heard it at the same time: a lamb bleating, and then another, and ewes answering their calls. Through a break in the clouds we saw one ewe start upward toward the peaks, hopefully to her lamb in the rocks. The next day the sun was shining and tiny lambs were gamboling around in the boulders and rock piles. We could only hope we hadn't lost any to the inclement weather the previous day.

In July 2004, history was made when the first wild release of desert bighorns in Coahuila State took place in the Carmens. The El Carmen crew, consisting of Billy Pat, Armando Galindo, Jonás Delgadillo Villalobos, Mauro Alonso, and myself, had made the long haul from El Carmen to Hermosillo, Sonora, about eighteen hundred miles. Alejandro Espinosa was waiting for us as well as the capture crew. We gathered at the Yaqui Reserve where a group of desert bighorns from an earlier capture at Isla del Tiburón had been for several years. Martin Franco and his crew had the drop nets in place and after we looked the location over, we came up with alternative strategies in case the first did not work. We were ready to drop the net the next morning.

The next morning was clear and hot, and the bighorns were coming in to water at a corral located at the bottom of a sheer mountain. We stayed well out of the way and let Martin work his magic. He dropped the net, and one ram hooked a horn in the corner of the net and several escaped. We would deal with them later. First we had to work the bighorns up under the net. Ivonne Cassigne, our veterinarian from Mexico City, was ready to begin taking samples for further testing, and everyone literally grabbed a bighorn and began untangling it. Blindfolds were quickly put on the bighorns and order restored. We radio-collared the sheep quickly, and in less than five minutes per sheep the samples were taken, collars were on, and the sheep were being loaded into the trailer.

Next on the agenda was to capture the escapees. The corral was set up so that the sheep could be driven from the hilly area down into an alley of sorts, and then have a gate shut behind them. Once in the smaller enclosure, it was simply a matter of catching the sheep, and getting a blindfold on it and working it up. This went quickly and soon they were all loaded in the trailer and we were on the road in less than two hours. Now came the hard part: the long haul back to Coahuila. We left Hermosillo and drove into Casas

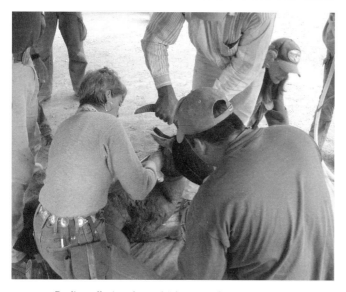

Radio collaring desert bighorns in Sonora, Mexico.
Photo B. P. McKinney, 2005

Grandes, Chihuahua. Then we left Casas Grandes at 6:30 a.m. and drove nonstop except for gasoline, arriving at El Carmen around 3:00 a.m. the morning of the third day. We checked the sheep, and they were fine. Then we pulled the trailer to the release site, and checked everything one more time. We took the two ewes and one lamb out of the smaller compartment of the trailer and held them so they could be released at the same time that the rams came out of the trailer, thus reducing the chance of them being separated from the group. The rams came first, thundering out of the trailer as if devil himself were after them. We simultaneously released the two ewes and the lamb so that they were directly behind the rams, and away they all went. I breathed a sigh of relief. They had traveled well and for the first time in over fifty years wild desert bighorns once again roamed the historic land in Coahuila.

This wasn't the end of the story. Permits from the Mexican government's wildlife agencies were in place for a final bighorn sheep capture at the Yaqui Reserve, and in late November 2004 we were once again on the road to Sonora. The weather was warm, and the helicopter crew were coming in to net gun the desert bighorns that remained at the Yaqui Reserve in Hermosillo. We were cleaning the reserve and taking all the sheep to the Carmens to augment the previous wild release. We needed more sheep, especially ewes, as we were ram heavy. The second day, which is the hardest of the trip, we left Sabinas and literally drove to the southern end of the Coahuila State and crossed into Durango, and then back into Coahuila for a few miles and then into Chihuahua. This road system is complicated to say the least. We had to drive all the way across the state of Chihuahua, up to the Arizona-Sonora border at Agua Prieta, and then head to Hermosillo. There is no other road to get to Hermosillo that we can pull the big trailer through. The Sierra Madre is a truly awe-inspiring mountain chain, and the winding mountain road that is the quickest way to Hermosillo does not permit any commercial vehicles or trailers. We drove all day, and late that night we pulled into Chihuahua City, managing to get lost only once in our quest for the Holiday Inn Express with a Denny's restaurant next door and a parking lot that the gooseneck trailer would fit in. The second morning we were up at 4:30 a.m. and on the road by 5:30 a.m. with another long day ahead of us. Before we reached Casas Grandes, we could see snow on the high mountain tops. Finally, we pulled into Agua Prieta and then hit the second of the mountain roads; in late afternoon we pulled into Hermosillo, Sonora.

Capture day dawned crisp and clear; I was anxious, hoping all would go well. The helicopter crew from New Zealand were awesome as usual; they always know their business, but did they ever have to work for these sheep. The cliffs are high, sheer, and full of palo blanco, saguaro cactus, cholla, caves, overhangs, and inclines so steep that it is almost impossible to stand up. We had our workstation set up, ready to go. When the first sheep comes in swinging below the helicopter it is time to go to work. Each sheep gets blindfolded, checked for parasites, has samples and temperature taken, injections given, and is radio collared. All data are recorded and then the animal is loaded in the trailer. We have all worked together long enough that all of us know our jobs and we usually can completely work up each bighorn sheep in five minutes or less. The quicker the better; once in the trailer the bighorns settle down quickly.

Inclement weather shut us down for half a day, so we concluded the capture on the second afternoon. Once the last sheep was in the trailer, the gate was shut and we were on the road home. We left Hermosillo at 3:30 p.m. in t-shirts, as the weather was sunny and warm, almost tropical. The sheep were in the gooseneck with Mauro driving, and Bill and I were in the second truck with a flat-bed trailer and five bighorns in specially built wooden crates. The farther we drove from Hermosillo toward Agua Prieta, the cooler the weather, and by dark it was cold.

Upon arrival in Agua Prieta, we discovered snow. Shortly we were on the dreaded Highway 2. The night was cold and still, the moon was up, and there were a couple of inches of snow on the ground but the road was okay. We drove steadily and finally stopped at Casas Grandes at 3:30 a.m., and the next evening we arrived in Torreón, Coahuila. The last day was a repeat, driving until well after dark. Bill got in the back seat of the truck to sleep a couple of hours, while I took a turn at the wheel. We stopped in Cuatro Ciénegas and Bill took over driving the gooseneck so that Mauro could sleep a few hours. I was wide awake, eager to get home. The Cuatro Ciénegas Basin was incredible, with the light of the full moon illuminating every cactus and bush, and the night was bitter cold. The sandy basins glittered like fine silver. Driving along, I was thinking to myself that never in a million years would I have ever dreamed that I would be pulling a trailer full of bighorns across the northern Coahuila desert in the wee hours of the morning.

Finally, we arrived at Sabinas, stopped for the final gas tank fill-up, and checked the bighorns. All the sheep were fine, not even a runny nose; they had traveled a lot better than we had. We drove through Múzquiz, deserted in the early morning. Never had the Maderas del Carmen looked so good; in the early morning light the peaks were sentinels that I had wanted to see for two days. We arrived in Pilares at 8:15 a.m. exhausted but elated. We had good sheep, they were in great condition, and shortly they would be on their way up the mountain. We drove to the release site and Bill opened the gate. The ewes and lambs came out first, followed by the rams. They hit the ground running and didn't stop until they were high in the rocks on the mountain. We were home, and the sheep were on the mountain, their radio collars beeping their locations. I had

visions of going home to a good cup of coffee and about twelve hours of sleep. But first, the trailer had to be cleaned out, hosed down, and disinfected, equipment unloaded, and sheep locations checked again. We got home at 4:00 p.m.

This group of sheep was needed to supplement the small group we had in the wild. Many of the ewes were pregnant, which meant that we could anticipate adding more numbers to the herd in a couple of months.

On March 17, 2005, the weather was cold and sunny, and high in the Maderas the mountain peaks were covered with snow. Jonás and I headed out to check the bighorns. We were watching two ewes that had moved into an area to lamb. There stood ewe #37 with her new lamb, the first lamb to be born in the wild in Coahuila in over fifty years. What a scene, a desert bighorn ewe and lamb standing on a rocky outcrop in the desert with the big mountain peaks behind them covered in snow. No, I didn't have a camera with me, but I will never forget the sight of the ewe with her tiny lamb that cold March morning. We called Bill on the radio, letting him know about the new lamb. We returned to Pilares that afternoon and I emailed everyone that the first lamb born in the wild in Coahuila in more than fifty years was doing well.

Capturing and transporting bighorns is exhausting work. You worry, you don't sleep, you drink cokes and eat junk food, you check and recheck equipment, you cool down hot sheep, you check them at every stop, you walk into a fancy hotel in dirty jeans and t-shirt and get funny looks, you wonder what you are doing at 4:00 a.m. in the morning in the middle of nowhere with a load of desert bighorns. But you know deep down why you do it, and you wouldn't trade places with anyone else. You see a big ram standing on a desert peak, or a tiny lamb curled up asleep at the base of an ocotillo, you see the future of a species that was extirpated and is now getting a second chance, and you know you would do it again and again, damn right you would.

We were old hands with the "Coahuila-Sonora Bighorn Run," and the third trip we made to Sonora on Highway 2 didn't really bother us that much. In November 2005 we were once again on the road, this time headed to Punto Cirios, northwest of Hermosillo. We drove to Torreón the first night, the second night we stopped at Agua Prieta, and the third afternoon we pulled into Hermosillo in time for a late lunch.

When we headed out to Punto Cirios, I was excited; hopefully we would get there in time to see the Sea of Cortez, as our ranch destination was right on the coast. Four hours later we arrived at the ranch, unloaded, and the sun was setting fast. The biologist working at the ranch told us we had time to go see the coast. We all loaded up in the back of the pickup and headed south. I couldn't imagine the coast being this close to the desert. The landscape was pure Sonoran Desert. Saguaro cactus, cholla, barrel cactus, and other brushy species of vegetation were all sparsely distributed over the red earth and rocky hills. We came around a corner and were stunned by the Sea of Cortez in a brilliant red and gold sunset. We scrambled out of the truck like kids at a carnival and headed to the beach. The water was crystal clear, and far across the water we could make out the outline of Baja Sur; and in the other direction, Isla del Tiburón, where many of our desert bighorns originated.

We searched for seashells, stuffing our pockets full, and then Hugo found whale bones, the first I had seen in the wild. I had no idea the ribs on a whale were so long; way over our head. Dark was fast approaching, but we were reluctant to leave. It was hard to imagine the desert running into the sea, but that is exactly what it does in this area of Sonora. The beach was little more than a narrow strip. Driving back, the sky was twinkling with stars, the crescent moon a sliver of pale gold. The air was crisp; I heard the last waves hit the beach as we turned the curve toward camp. I was secretly hoping that maybe the sheep wouldn't go under the net in the morning and we could have an entire day to explore the beach, take photos, and enjoy this marvelous area of desert and sea.

Before daylight the next morning, we had coffee and breakfast, although just coffee for me, as I get the jitters before we capture. I inhale my coffee and wait to eat breakfast much later. The morning air was crisp, the desert was slowly waking up with the pale rose dawn. Gambel's quail were calling and marching along like soldiers in a line, headed to water or to a favorite feeding spot. Say's phoebes were flitting about camp, a resident pair apparently having claimed the camp house for their own. We checked equipment, and headed to the capture site. Work-up was fast, and we were loaded and on the road by 9:00 a.m. As we headed back toward Hermosillo, I thought about the sea and the desert coming together, and I could imagine the desert bighorns standing on the rocky outcrops above the pounding surf, water everywhere but not to drink. I would love to come back and visit this area again, when there is time to explore, enjoy the sunset, swim in the sea, collect shells, bird watch, and maybe even see whales.

Desert bighorns are the rulers of the high and dry desert peaks with scorching hot winds, little vegetation, rock piles, and boulder-strewn slopes. Today in Coahuila, the desert bighorn is once again roaming the high red-rock peaks where they historically occurred. It is only through the efforts of many people that the desert bighorn is back in Coahuila. CEMEX, Agrupación Sierra Madre, Unidos para la Conservación, a host of government agencies in Mexico, the Texas Parks and Wildlife Department, Texas Bighorn Society, and Wild Sheep Foundation are all players in the world of the desert bighorn.

There was no "Coahuila sheep team" when Bill and I moved to Coahuila. We had worked with bighorns in Texas for many years, and we brought our experience and the crew here got jump-started on desert bighorns. Today the team is comprised of Billy Pat McKinney, Jonás Delgadillo Villalobos, Hugo Sotelo, Beto Martinez, Mauro Alonso, Armando Galindo, and myself here at El Carmen, with Alejandro Espinosa and Dan Roe in Monterrey, and Ivonne Cassigne, our veterinarian in Mexico City. We have formed a team that works well together, and we have worked sheep in Coahuila, Sonora, and Chihuahua. There are other players and they are important and appreciated. The project's crew members here at El Carmen, supervised by Salvador Villarreal, help tremendously in the day-to-day management of desert bighorns, developing watering places high on the desert peaks, maintaining pipelines, and a host of other work that makes our job easier.

The future looks bright for the desert bighorn in northern Mexico. In September 2009 our survey of the population inside the criadero numbered over 250, with additional sheep in the wild. Several months later in December 2009, we captured twenty ewes and ten rams from inside the criadero and released them on the mountains with the existing wild population. One day in the future, maybe the near future, we will see desert bighorns from Texas and Coahuila mixing. One of the benefits of this mix is building strong genetic diversity within these populations. The desert bighorns are back in historic range and hopefully populations in both countries will continue to grow, remaining an integral part of the flora and fauna for many generations to come.

In February 2010, Billy Pat, Alejandro Espinosa, and I headed to Reno, Nevada for the Wild Sheep Foundation Convention, the first time a tag from Coahuila had been offered for the sale of one sheep permit. Sheep conservation requires incredible amounts of money, and through the sale of tags, funding goes toward the sheep project to enable us to build more water developments, buy radio collars, and capture and transport sheep. A tag for one old ram helps many sheep. Sportsmen hunting bighorns have provided many millions of dollars, allowing many sheep programs in the southwestern United States, to continue their restoration programs. If the phone rang, and I was told we were needed in Sonora in two days to capture sheep, you bet I would be ready to go, and so would the rest of the crew. Everything would be loaded, equipment checked, and we would head out before daylight, already dreading Highway 2 but elated to be capturing desert bighorns to build the Coahuila herd.

As I wrote this in March 2010, I was excited to be counting tiny lambs while they bucked and jumped from rock to rock on the high peaks, suddenly dropping down on the boulders for a quick nap in the sun. They are the future, and I hope that they will continue to flourish.

13 The Road to Campo Uno

The road to Campo Uno is an example of a lesson in vegetation and elevation. Leaving Campo Cinco the road winds upward for several kilometers heading east. To the left is the junction of the road that leads to a great overlook: this area is known as El Divisadero (The Divide). El Divisadero is diverse—even though you have climbed upward, the vegetation changes abruptly here from a predominantly pine-fir forest at Campo Cinco to a pine-oak woodland. A few firs are on the highest ridge tops, but oaks and pines rule. The soil also changes to a red, sandy loam. Here you start the descent to reach Campo Uno. As you leave El Divisadero, the terrain levels out for a short distance through park-like oak and pine woodland with open areas of native grasses interspersed with wildflowers. This area is one of the best places in the Carmens to see wild turkey.

The road twists and winds, climbing and then spiraling downward to El Salero, which is predominantly oak woodland with pines on the ridge tops. To the east, the Serranías del Burro are visible, to the south the Encantada range is a soft blue, and in the north, the Loma de Colorado looks like a series of tiny hills. Below you glimpse the road winding toward Campo Uno. Butterflies, wildflowers, oaks, and birds all abound in this area. The ever-present Mexican jays call raucously as they spot intruders in their territory. Montezuma quail are numerous, as they prefer the open park-like areas to feed on the tubers of wood sorrel and other plants. It is always a surprise when these harlequin-faced quail explode from underfoot, flying a short distance and then squatting, hoping they are hidden.

One day in late September the fog was thick, and I stopped my four-wheeler to readjust equipment. As I stepped off the machine I heard a bird call that I wasn't familiar with. The fog was dense and swirling close to the ground, and I couldn't see much in the trees, but the sound appeared to be coming from very close by, a call note with a tiny squawk at the end. I remained perfectly still; in just a few seconds I heard the call again, even closer. What could this be? Suddenly I saw a tiny chick, and then another and another, six in all, not three feet in front of the four-wheeler in the middle of the road. They were all milling around, apparently separated from the adults. I remained perfectly still, hoping the adults would come back for them. This was a late hatch—the chicks were only a couple of days old, tiny little puffballs of brown and cream feathers. In their confusion, they uttered the call ending in a tiny squawk. Seconds passed and I heard the low whistle of one of the adults. Activity picked up with the chicks as they began scurrying toward the whistle. They crossed the road and I saw the adult male only a few feet away. Had he been there the entire time, afraid to go to the chicks because of my presence, or had he just arrived looking for his lost brood? The reunion was a happy one with much calling. Then as if to say, "Okay, kids, enough, let's go," the male led them away into the thicker grasses.

I didn't get a photo of the chicks, as I didn't want to scare them and see them scatter in all directions. Here in the Carmens the Montezuma quail is doing well—they are found in a variety of elevations and habitats, all of which have similar species of plants, water sources, and cover, and all sites are protected. Chick mortality may be high because of their reluctance to fly. Bobcats and foxes are probably the main predators, followed by the resident Cooper's hawks and northern goshawks.

Near the end of El Salero, there is a road that turns abruptly to the right. Following along this road, you are treated to a pristine, predominantly pine woodland with oaks scattered throughout. A small spring-fed stream meanders along the canyon. This stream has many natural tinajas that hold rainwater when flow from the spring is low or absent. I always want to be silent in this area, listening to the pine needles rustling in the wind, hearing the cry of a pair of zone-tailed hawks, and surprising a bear as he ambles along. The road winds upward and then tops out—this is the Puerta Linces. The view is astonishing: Chamiceras and Fronteriza are below, and if I could see over the big hill, my house would be visible in Cañón el Álamo. Winds must be fierce here, as the junipers are gnarled and twisted from many years of punishing north winds. Plains prickly pear and magueys grow sparsely along the ridge top; the vegetation thickens as it slopes to the canyon bottoms. Bears use this area as a travel corridor from the mid-elevation canyons up to the high country, elk feed on the slopes below, and butterflies catch the wind on this high ridge, floating effortlessly southward.

Back to our journey to Campo Uno. Leaving El Salero we wind downward into the canyon complex known as Cañón Carboneras. The canyon head is an open grassy area where painted redstarts flit from tree to tree and muddy spots on the road host a large variety of butterflies. Remains of Indian camps are evidenced by the many chippings and broken arrowheads found here. The canyon narrows abruptly and becomes rocky; a mountain stream crosses the road too many times to count. When rains are abundant, in this section of the canyon rushing water roils over the many boulders, creating mini-waterfalls, dropping into deep pools. At times we have crossed the creek with water rising over the front end of the four-wheelers. Once when the creek was high, I crossed in the morning, and then in the afternoon when I returned the water had risen considerably. My husband crossed in his four-wheel-drive truck and assured me that I could cross as well. I turned the wheels upstream and forded the creek with water running thigh high on the four-wheeler.

Black hawks and zone-tail hawks are summer residents and can usually be seen on a daily basis in this area. Black bears splash and cool off in the pools, and Mexican primroses, cardinal flowers, native ferns, grasses, and willows line the stream banks. The many sheer cliffs are natural rock gardens with magueys, succulents, mosses, and lichens growing in cracks and crevices. Just around the bend in the road the canyons open. If it has been raining, you see a breathtaking waterfall. High above, it pours downward to the canyon bottom, entering a rock chute and finally flowing into the main stream.

Farther down the canyon, we continue following the creek in its downward path toward Campo Uno. In May through October, this canyon is a butterfly paradise. Hairstreaks, sulphurs, painted ladies, west coast ladies, swallowtails, Arizona

Waterfall on the road to Campo Uno, 2005

Presa (dam) at Campo Uno, 2005

sisters, ground-streaks, mini-streaks, Mexican yellows, Mexican silverspots, and many more feed on nectar from the many wildflowers, particularly the milkweed species. The canopy is dense, with sunlight filtering through in patches here and there. Basswood trees are common in this area. Many oak species, ponderosa pines, dogwood, madroño, point-leaf manzanita, ninebark, and a host of other species all contribute to the wide diversity in plant life.

One last twisting downward curve past an anonymous grave on the left, cross the creek twice more, and ahead you can see an opening in the woodland. The road is smooth, you turn one last curve, and you are at Campo Uno.

The first time I visited Campo Uno, the remains of a large lumber camp, including a steam engine, corrals, and several old houses, were still there. A lone chimney in the charred remains of a house seemed to be a sentinel of times past. A large dam had been constructed here many years ago to hold water for the camp and logging operations. The dam needed repair, and several cottonwoods were dotted around the small lake created by the dam. After years of logging operations here, the bottom of the lake was composed of sawdust. Who knew how deep it was? Still, it was a peaceful area, and the view up canyon magnificent. The water that spilled over the dam wound down the canyon and flowed into Cañón Botella, and from there flowed down to the east side of the Maderas, coming out at El Club, and then flowing farther onto the grasslands near Ejido Morelos. Much of the high country in the Carmens is owned by Alberto Garza Santos, a conservation-minded landowner who bought the high country with the intention of preserving it. The El Carmen Project has a long-term conservation agreement with Alberto to manage the land and wildlife.

Standing in the sunshine on one of my first trips to Campo Uno, I could imagine the hustle and bustle of the logging camp, saws whining, children running and playing around the houses, and horses stamping in the corral, swishing their tails at annoying deer flies. But I also saw the aftermath of rubble, trash, plastic bottles, glass, old tin, falling-down shacks, and a small lake full of sawdust. The dam was going to be repaired along with general clean-up in the area. One night the men working there cleaning up and building the cabin heard a terrific noise in the night—they rushed outside to see a tremendous flash flood brought on by heavy rain in the higher elevations. The breakage of the dam was a sight to see: tree trunks, entire trees, debris of every description, and huge boulders all came down from the high canyons to land in the small lake.

The lake was cleaned, the years of sawdust removed, and the dam rebuilt. Alberto built a modern log cabin for his family. El Carmen guests also use the cabin. The old steam boiler at the lake edge rests on a red-brick foundation that continues in place, a reminder of the past.

I am a hopeless packrat of all things antique, and so I too have reminder of the old logging camp. One day Jonás and I were here checking acorn production, and we started looking around the old home site with the burned chimney. He found a hand-forged butterfly, made of heavy metal. It is part of my collection of antiques from the Carmens, along with tin cups, old frying pans, enamel coffeepots, and many other small treasures from the past.

In the early morning, the sun's rays touch the peaks high above Uno and the sierras are reflected in the lake. Ducks spend the winter here, and black bear and Carmen Mountain white-tails water here. Hoary bats are abundant, flying over the lake at dusk catching insects. Butterflies cover the muddy areas, leopard frogs and canyon tree frogs begin their chorus at dusk. Sleeping here at night you hear the water flowing over the dam into the streambed below.

In the past this area was not only logged, but hunted and overgrazed. Hunters at El Club hiked into the area to hunt bear and deer. The logging operation took a heavy toll on the habitat and wildlife, but it is recovering rapidly. Grasses are coming back in areas that were overgrazed, deer numbers are rebounding, and the black bear population in this area is growing rapidly. Campo Uno will retain its historic name, but it is now an area rich in biodiversity, one of the Carmens' jewels.

I will always remember November 2001. We had been in Coahuila a little more than a month and Bill was busy with operations and projects. Four new biologists and I were beginning the first long-term baseline inventory of the flora and fauna in the Carmens. The old headquarters of Rancho Pilares served as the base for all operations. Our office stayed the same temperature whether the wide sliding metal door was open or closed. Equipment was stacked on shelves and our computers were set up on a single table. This was a temporary office until we could get repairs and renovations completed on what had been a small house that was part of the old headquarters building. November was a very busy month and unusually cold for late fall. I had assigned different projects to various biologists and we were all helping each other until we had the projects established. Small mammal trapping, bird observation and point counts, and vegetation transects and mapping were being conducted simultaneously.

November 28 was cold, twenty-nine degrees in the office and outside. Jonás and I left Pilares and headed up Cañón el Álamo to Cañón Juárez to set out fifty small mammal traps. We remarked how cold it was. The clouds had been building up and by noon the sky was lead gray, looking like rain. Just before the entrance to Cañón Juárez we saw a large male bear walking up the mountain; we stopped and watched him through binoculars until he went over the top of the ridge. I remarked that he was probably looking for a cave or old mine to den up in until the cold front passed.

We continued on until we reached the middle of the arroyo that comes down the canyon. The arroyo was dry; seeds were abundant on grasses growing along the banks. Pine-oak woodland begins in this area, and the oaks, big-tooth maples, and shrubs were brilliant slashes of color, with red, orange, and yellow interspersed with the green of the pines. The color of the leaves contrasted sharply with the dark gray sky. We decided to set out the trap line here to determine which small mammals were resident in the area. The temperature had not warmed up all day and the wind was bitter and out of the north. We saw red-naped and Williamson's sapsuckers, black-crested titmice, Mexican jays, and many chipping and white-crowned sparrows. High overhead a red-tailed hawk soared over the crags—he was hunting early, maybe he knew a storm was headed our way. We hiked back to the truck and hot coffee, and then headed down canyon, stopping once to check bear scratches on a huge madroño tree. The bear obviously used this tree on a regular basis, as many old and new scratches were cut into the light-colored wood. Farther down the canyon we stopped at Casa San Isidro. Bill and I would be moving here as soon as the renovation and new additions were finished on the house. I was anxious to move in, as we would remain camped out in a small bedroom at Pilares until the house was complete. We arrived back at Pilares about 5:00 p.m. Pilares was as cold as the upper canyon and the wind just as bitter. At midnight, I went outside to check the weather: it was bitter cold, windy, and sleeting like crazy.

Back inside and shivering, I snuggled down in the covers listening to the sleet falling on the tin roof. The next morning about 7:00 a.m., we were all heading in to breakfast, and there was no sleet, with an even light gray sky. I remarked that it sure looked like snow, and Bill said that the air felt heavy with moisture and that it likely would snow. We were still at breakfast when the first huge snowflakes started falling. What a surprise—snow in the lower desert elevations is always unexpected. The flakes were huge, the delicate patterns resembling white lace against a lead-gray backdrop. We assumed that perhaps a heavy flurry was underway, but the snow continued to fall at a rate of one inch per hour.

Bill, Jonás, and I took the truck and headed to Cañón Juárez. The snow was even heavier here than in Pilares and still falling steadily. Bill let us out at the beginning of the mammal line and said he would pick us up at the end. We stumbled over rocks and brush in the creek bed; finding the traps was difficult as they were all covered with snow. My hands were freezing and my feet wet and cold. We loaded all the traps and headed back down the canyon. One more stop—we had been mist-netting and banding birds at Tanque de los Fresnos and had furled all the nets the day before.

Today, they were drooped, full of ice and snow, and a mess. We tried to shake off as much snow and ice as possible from six nets and bag them. It didn't take long, but we were both shivering in the cold. All I could think about was a hot cup of coffee at Pilares. Finally, we had all the equipment and drove down the canyon to Pilares. The canyon was so quiet—perhaps even the ever-present Mexican jays were so surprised at the unexpected snow that it left them speechless, or squawkless. Few birds were moving; I saw a handful of vesper sparrows perched in bushes and a ruby-crowned kinglet.

Snow in the Carmens, 2001. Photo J. D. Villalobos, 2001

We arrived back at Pilares, where the office was still freezing cold, and unloaded all the wet equipment. We couldn't believe it—still snowing at noon, and at 5:00 p.m. there was exactly one foot of snow at Pilares, which is around 1300 meters elevation. I figured it was probably a meter deep in the high country, as the mountain was completely covered. We took photos, the guys built a snowman that had a remarkable resemblance to a former employee. We watched as darkness settled over the landscape, accompanied by total silence and a cold twenty-two degrees. Bill called the Monterrey office, and of course, they could not believe it was snowing in Pilares, much less an accumulation of twelve inches. We sent them a photo.

The next morning it was a winter wonderland—the sun shone brightly, the sky was bright blue, and everything was encrusted with dia-monds. The biologist and I headed out in the truck to take photos, see what was moving, and marvel at the snow. We went to the criadero first; desert bighorn tracks in the snow were unusual, to say the least. We saw several bighorns standing on rim rocks, and all the telemetry signals were live. I could imagine what they were thinking, having come from the Sonoran Desert. We checked the dirt tanks and discovered not a single duck, when two days ago the tanks had been filled with diverse species, including ring-necks, canvasbacks, mallards, buffleheads, lesser scaup, pied-billed grebes, northern pintail, northern shoveler, green-winged, and cinnamon teal. They must have flown out before the storm hit, and were probably somewhere south where it was much warmer. The earthen tanks were beautiful, the water was shimmering, the sky reflected in the water, and all around covered with snow. We saw a black-tailed jackrabbit sitting under a creosote bush; apparently he thought he was hidden. We took photos from two feet away and he never moved. Scaled quail were perched in the tops of bushes as if to say, "Enough, that stuff is cold!"

By mid-afternoon, the sun was melting much of the snow. We were headed to Morteros and to my utter amazement there were nine ring-billed gulls on the paved airstrip at Pilares. They were walking around on the pavement, which was bare of snow. I wondered where they blew in from, as the nearest lake with gulls was near Sabinas at Presa Don Martin, which was southeast of us some four hours away. The storm came out of the north, so maybe they flew from West Texas at Balmorrhea Lake. They were definitely out of their element in the desert lowlands, walking around on the airstrip.

By 5:00 p.m. the temperature was dropping, icicles were beginning to form from the melting snow dripping off the roof. By dark it was twenty-two degrees and the icicles were huge. Another cold night in the desert. I wondered if all the wildlife had found shelter, those birds with fluffed-up feathers perched in bushes and trees.

That was the biggest snow in ten years. The melting snow put moisture in the ground that was needed for the spring greening. We had an incredible winter wonderland for one day. While slushing through the mud the next couple of days, we were still talking about the wild snow storm. Since then we have had several light snows but nothing to compare with the twelve inches on November 28, 2001.

Three feet of snow fell on the high mountain, and some areas probably more. Shortly thereafter another storm blew in from the north and we had a terrific ice storm—tree branches were broken, and trees were blown over with bare roots exposed. Pine limbs broke like matchsticks, and the road was blocked in many places. The winds must have been gale force in the high country.

In the winter of 2001, storms blowing in and out, cold rains, fog, sleet, light snows, and ice were normal rather than unusual. Since then we have often wished for another deep snow to provide winter moisture for the flora and fauna and a winter wonderland for us.

One of my favorite places in the Carmens is Cañón Juárez, especially in the autumn when the foliage on the big-tooth maples, oaks, and Virginia creeper vines presents a collage of gold, red, orange, and green. Cañón Juárez begins just past our house in Cañón el Álamo where the canyon forks, right into Juárez and left into the Cañón Fronteriza. Cañón Juárez itself is narrow, following a creek bed with intermittent pools of clear water. The sides are limestone, steep, and covered with pine and oak. The creek bed is lined with oaks and big-tooth maple, wildflowers, and huge boulders.

Cañón Juárez and Cañón el Álamo contain populations of a cactus species that may reach the northern limit of its range here in the Carmens. *Viejito* (old one) is its common name, and the scientific name, *Echinocereus longisetus*. This species grows in isolated clumps amid limestone rocks and crevices and on cliff overhangs. The viejito forms large clumps, and the plant body is completely covered in long, soft white spines. In late spring and early summer, the buds form, and then the flowers open—large showy magenta blooms that are a sharp contrast to the white spines covering the plant. These plants are numerous in the two canyons, but are not considered common. Rather, they are scattered about, one here and one there. Honeybees work the blooms for nectar, and later the fruits are pinkish-brown. Javelina, notorious for uprooting cactus and feeding on

(right) Viejito cactus in
Cañón Juárez, 2003
(below) Virginia creeper in
Cañón Juárez, 2003

their succulent roots, pass this cactus by, which is good because it is not common and is very widely distributed. This species also grows south of the Carmens in the adjacent Sierra Encantada to the west, where it is also scattered in distribution. Because the lands in the Carmens are protected, perhaps one day this species will become common.

Cañon Juárez was overgrazed for many years by goats, cattle, and horses, and one of our biggest management problems was trespassing cattle from the nearby ejido. Finally, the only effective solution turned out to be fencing the high country to keep the cattle out. Grasses are coming back fast now that the land is being rested.

This canyon is diverse in plants and birdlife; the pools of water are oases for birds and provide water to all wildlife in the area. Near the upper end of the canyon a road forks to the right and climbs upward several miles to the Mesa de los Fresnos, a vast mesa covered with native grasses interspersed with juniper, giant daggers, and other shrubs.

At the point where the road forks to the Mesa de los Fresnos is the site of the old Casa Juárez, named for Mexican President Benito Juárez (1806–1872), who reportedly spent the night here. The house is made from rock, with dirt floors, and has sheltered many vaqueros, goat herders, bats, and packrats. Here the canyon widens, the road wanders through a grassy flat—a favorite travel route for black bears—and black

hawks nest along the creek. In the upper reaches of the canyon the creek runs year-round unless it is extremely dry. Water sources include several springs, and the water is clear and icy cold. There are no native fish in the Carmens, but the pools are teeming with leopard frogs. At the far end of the canyon, a set of corrals with dipping vats were once located on a small knoll. The corrals and vats were removed and the area cleaned up.

Since this area was already disturbed (i.e., much of the native vegetation was gone due to previous constructions and livestock operations), in 2003 we built a set of soft-release pens for the Rocky Mountain elk that we planned to locate in the Carmens in March. We had conducted habitat surveys, a literature search, established vegetation transects, built exclosures to monitor vegetation and habitat use, and obtained the permits for the capture of the elk. Our good friend and partner in the elk project, David Garza Lagüera, was supplying the elk from his herd at Rancho Rincón in the adjacent Serranías del Burro. These elk were acclimated to Coahuila and healthy, our first choice for the Carmens. Several previous attempts to introduce elk into this area had poor results. We decided to use the soft-release method, which entails putting the captured elk into the pens for a certain period of time during which they are monitored. This enables the animals to develop site and herd fidelity. We planned to place the captured elk in the pen and provide food and water for thirty days, at which time the gate would be opened and the elk allowed to leave on their own.

The capture went smoothly and the elk were placed in the pen without mishap. Jonás, Feliciano, Beto, and I were feeding and watering the elk twice daily during their time in the pen. The weather was cold and sunny for the most part, but one day in particular it was bitterly cold; we were putting out hay and pellets, the wind was howling and in a matter of minutes the sky was completely overcast. First it started sleeting, followed by snow flurries, wind, and then rain, and the sun and calm returned, all in about twenty minutes. We couldn't believe how much weather we saw in that short time period.

While the elk were in the pens at Juárez, Bill suggested we sow native grass seeds in the pens. With the hoof action from the elk the seeds would be pushed into the soil, and once they were released the area could serve as an exclosure, protected from the trespassing livestock from the ejido, and we could see how quickly the seeds would re-vegetate this old corral site. We sowed blue grama, sprangletop, plains bristlegrass, and side-oats grama in early March 2003. This area is now covered in grass and no sign of the old corral remains.

We had planned to quietly open the gate and let the elk wander out, which they did, with minor changes. Many organizations were involved in the elk project: CEMEX, Museo Maderas del Car-men A.C., Agrucapión Sierra Madre, Comisión Nacional de Áreas Naturales Protegidas, Secretaría del Medio Ambiente, Recursos Naturales y Pesca, Instituto Coahuilense de Ecología-Gobierno de Coahuila, Unidos para la Conservación, Procuraduría Federal de Protección al Ambiente, Instituto Nacional de Ecología, Rancho Rincón, and the El Carmen staff. Everyone wanted to see the elk leave the corral, including newspaper reporters, people from the aforementioned organizations, and many others. We shuttled everyone up to the pens. The elk were nervous, walking about and flicking their ears. We didn't want them to panic, so we had everyone move back from the corrals and stay in the surrounding trees and brush. Bill positioned several people at the west end of the pens and Jonás and I opened the gate and began calling to the elk, shaking the feed bag. This is not normal procedure on a soft release. You normally open the gate and leave the area, letting the animals move out at their own pace. The gate is left open for several days, or longer, allowing the animals to come and go if they wish. Our situation was a little different, since people wanted photos of the elk coming out of the pens, and we wanted them to leave the corrals quietly and not be spooked into running. Our objective was to keep the elk in this area as a herd and prevent them from scattering.

I was as nervous as the elk, as we continued calling and shaking the feed sack. The elk were accustomed to us feeding them, but they could smell the other people. Finally, after about ten minutes, a particularly gentle cow that loved the pelleted feed came forward and walked slowly out of the pen, and then the rest of the group, not wanting to be left out of their daily ration of pellets, followed. They didn't spook, but moved up the canyon, which is basically where we wanted them to go. I breathed a sigh of relief. Everyone got their photos and the project was featured in several newspapers, including in Mexico City.

The elk settled in the mid-elevation canyons, and are proving to be a good management tool in places where brush species had encroached on native grass areas, a direct result of domestic livestock overgrazing the area for many years. Currently the elk herd numbers eighty to one hundred individuals. Part of the herd is radio-collared to allow us to monitor their movement and habitat use. The elk have not been detrimental to any habitat thus far. They wander the canyons and high country in several groups, and in the fall they congregate in a number of areas. In late September, bulls bugling are common, especially in the Chamiceras area.

Another day that same month we had just finished feeding the elk and were returning to the truck when both of us saw the solitary eagle. We watched as it soared high above the cliffs and then turned and flew back toward Cañón Temblores. This was a new bird record for the Car-

mens, as the species had not been previously recorded here, but had been documented in the nearby Serranías del Burro by Aldegundo Garza de León in the early 1960s. Chabela Sellers and I had observed a pair on her ranch in the Burros in the 1990s when we were conducting a project to document the birdlife in this unique area. Jonás had also seen this species in the Burros in the 1990s. The solitary eagle is rare in northern Coahuila, and the species is evidently expanding its range. We have not documented their nesting, but in mid-March the eagles return and we see them in Juárez each spring and summer. We have also observed them near Campo Cinco and Campo Uno in the higher elevations. They are huge, bigger than golden eagles, and remind me of flying ironing boards. These birds are much bigger than the common black hawk and zone-tailed hawk, both of which are found in the Carmens during spring and summer. The field marks on the solitary eagle are the broad wings, large size, yellow feet, and white-banded tail. With the protection of the lands and ecological corridors here in northern Coahuila it is very possible that one day this species will expand its range into western Texas.

Cañón Juárez is an excellent example of how land can regenerate native vegetation after decades of continuous overgrazing by cattle, horses, and goats. For the first time in many years, the canyon bottoms and grassy park-like areas have knee-high native grasses. The cottonwood trees that remain are old, and the continued trampling in the creek bed has prevented new trees from growing. We have plans to replant native saplings so that the former riparian area of cottonwoods along the creek will once again provide nest sites for songbirds and raptors, and in the fall the leaves will rustle softly like falling rain and turn the creek bottoms to gold.

16 Zacatosa

Located at the lowest elevations in the project area, Zacatosa is comprised of typical desert floor habitat. Part of the old Rancho Pilares, Zacatosa is hot and sparsely vegetated with many areas of erosion. It is also an area rich in birdlife because of the earthen tanks that hold water and provide rest stops for migrating ducks, shore-birds, and a host of songbirds. Resident birds also nest in the vegetation surrounding the tanks. Several of these "dirt tanks"—crafted by humans—are scattered across the Zaca-tosa flats.

The soil in the Zacatosa flats is sandy, highly eroded, dotted with blackbrush, creosote bush, pitaya cactus, prick-ly pear, and tasajillo. In January 2006, I was driving down the road toward the gate that opens onto the road to Boquil-las. Valer Austin and I were headed to La Noria de Boquillas to sketch the towering escarpment above the village. I just happened to look out the truck window and saw an unusual cactus, so rare here in the northernmost limit of its range, that only one other plant had been recorded in 2001. We had searched many areas for this cactus and probably driv-en by this particular specimen on the road to the gate a hundred times. How did we miss it? It stood out like a sore thumb, the only plant in the area, and there were no other plants nearby. We stopped and I photographed the plant. How could only two plants be here and not elsewhere in the lower desert flats?

Tanque Zacatosa, 2006

The next day Jonás and I returned to the area with camera, ruler, and a small circle shaped fence to surround the cactus so that javelinas or other wildlife wouldn't uproot it or have it for lunch. I could key it to genus *Coryphantha*, but I had no idea about its species. We wrote a detailed description, took more photos, and decided to send it to José Guadalupe, a friend and expert on Mexican cactus. We received a reply in due time, and he identified it as *Coryphantha poselgeriana*, known as manca caballo. We searched the flats, walking miles looking for more, but have had no luck. How could two specimens of a cactus be so isolated and how did they get here? There are no smaller specimens growing near the plant, so reproduction by seeds is apparently not occurring. How long will this specimen live? The first specimen is dead, while the second appears to be robust and healthy. We found a single dried bloom; the seeds are tiny and brownish. We have not found this species in other areas adjacent to the project area, and the Mexican field guides indicate that it is found in several northern states, Coahuila included.

The dirt tank at Zacatosa holds water year-round, unless it is extremely dry, thus providing an oasis in the desert for wildlife and birds. In the early morning, the air is filled with sounds of songbirds, particularly in spring and summer. Varied and painted buntings, northern mockingbirds, loggerhead shrikes, Say's phoebe, ash-throated flycatchers, blue grosbeaks, northern

cardinals, pyrrhuloxia, black-throated sparrows, yellow-breasted chats, killdeer, mourning and white-winged doves, western kingbirds, vermilion flycatchers, black phoebe, Bell's vireo, curve-billed and crissal thrashers, verdins, Scott's orioles, and Mexican mallards are all common in spring and summer. In September, the first blue-winged teal come in from the north, followed by American wigeon, gadwall, northern pintail, lesser scaup, ring-necked duck, common goldeneye, bufflehead, northern shoveler, canvasback, and redhead. If the tank contains sufficient water and

Coryphantha cactus, 2006

Foothills of the Carmens, 2005

Young red-tailed hawk, 2008

Black bear in the Carmens. Photo J.D. Villalobos, 2004

Bear grass and Maderas peaks, 2004

Sunset yuccas, 2005

Clouds over Pico Centinela, 2005

Desert bighorn ram.
Photo S.G. Isern, 2010

Boletus mushrooms in pine-oak woodland.
Photo J.D. Villalobos, 2008

Fall color in the Carmens, 2010

Pico Loomis, highest point in the Sierra del Carmen. Photo B.P. McKinney, 2006

Sunset on the Carmens, 2008

Los Pilares, 2009

Los Pilares headquarters, 2009

Black bear, Marina, asleep in oak tree, 2008

Mule deer with fawn, 2008

El Carmen sheep team, Punto Cirios, Sonora, Mexico, 2005

Mountain meadow in high country, 2005

Puma with deer kill. Photo J.D. Villalobos, 2003

Red agave bloom, 2003

Sunset on El Jardín rim, 2008

Flying the Carmens with Vico in an ultralight.
Photo J.D. Villalobos, 2005

Bonnie McKinney and radio-collared black bear, Porfirio.
Photo J.D. Villalobos, 2004

food sources, many of these species winter here. If they are disturbed, they fly a short distance to the Tanque Lobo, returning to the Tanque Zacatosa as soon as we leave. Occasionally we see sandhill cranes and Canada geese flying overhead.

Santiago, Jonás, and I were checking the tanks for late migrants in May 2002 when we spotted a Swainson's hawk flying overhead and calling loudly. She flew directly to a mesquite near another tank in this area. We watched as she apparently checked on chicks in the nest. She flew when we approached, and Jonás and Santiago quickly climbed the tree; two chicks were in the nest, little fluff balls of white down. We had the banding equipment in the truck, so we rigged a cloth bag with a rope so Santiago could lower the chicks to us. We weighed, measured, and banded both chicks. Swainson's hawks are common here in the spring and summer. They are also among the species that perform a long fall migration to South America, returning here in late March and early April. We placed the chicks back in the nest and moved away from the nest site. Both the male and female returned to the area quickly, and the female landed at the nest and checked the chicks. Later that year in October, we watched a huge kettle of Swainson's hawks in the grasslands on the east side of the Carmens. The kettle of several hundred individuals spiraled lazily upward and south, and our eyes were riveted until they were out of sight.

Directly across from Tanque Zacatosa is a rocky hill where prickly pear, ocotillo, and pitaya grow in profusion among the rocks and boulders. This area is a favorite perch for a resident pair of red-tails. Many times in winter we see a pair perched side by side on ocotillo branches. The nest is below in the rocks, well guarded by the two adults. The Carmens have a large population of red-tailed hawks, and they range from the low desert to the highest peaks. In September and October when the red-tails move in from the north, we can always identify our birds from the migrants; ours are darker and slightly smaller than the red-tails that come from the northern United States. The resident red-tails become highly agitated when their northern cousins arrive; they dive at and chase the intruders, defending their territories. Order is restored in a couple of days and they settle down to their daily activities of hunting mice and small mammals, and perching in the sun on the ocotillos.

Shorebird migration appears to be heavier on the east side of the Carmens than on the west. On the west side, our records include long-billed dowitcher, long-billed curlew, white-faced ibis, great egret, great-blue heron, snowy egret, cattle egret, black-crowned night heron, green heron, sora, black-necked stilt, American avocet, least sandpiper, spotted sandpiper, solitary sandpiper, willet (rare), Wilson's phalarope, and a few other species. We never see large groups; normally one or two individuals at a tank work the mud flats.

Future fieldwork on the east side will no doubt add species to our list. The east side has many more migrants moving up the Valle de los Venados, which separates the Carmens and the Serranías del Burro.

By early 2011, much of the Zacatosa scrub and overgrazed areas had been restored to native grasslands; the area is now habitat for the reintroduced pronghorns. The Zacatosa area had been quite depleted of ground cover and erosion was very prominent. With rest and aeration using a tractor and Lawson aerator—which rolls over the hard-packed eroded ground, breaking the top crust with a series of dull spikes to allow rainfall to be absorbed into the ground—the native seed bank has regenerated, and the area has literally been transformed from a baked desert flat to historical grassland.

17 La Cachuchua

There is only one passable road to the high country of the Carmens, also known as the Maderas. The road is on the west side and leaves from Los Pilares. Departing the lower desert country, the climb is gradual. The peaks tower above and first-time visitors to the Maderas probably have second thoughts about schlepping up the mountain in a vehicle. Although the road is good, you must have four-wheel drive to make it to the top.

The road meanders along and winds through the mid-elevation landscape dominated by sotol and yucca, and gradually you enter the oaks and juniper, still climbing steadily. The road passes by Los Cojos, the site of an old fluorspar mining operation, and the remains of a rock house down in the canyon are visible. The view from Los Cojos is breathtaking: to the northwest is Big Bend National Park, and to the west Chihuahua, where the high jagged peaks of the Sierra de Hechiceros are barely visible. The Sierra Santa Fé del Pino is to the south and in between is a series of smaller mountains surrounded by desert.

Leaving Los Cojos, you begin to climb steadily—the grade is steep, the road is carved into the mountain. To your left a large, deep arroyo reminds you to pay attention to your driving. You round a curve and face a very steep grade with a sharp curve at the top; this is first-gear, low-range four-wheel driving. You grind slowly upward, make the turn, bounce over some protruding rock ledges, and are con-

La Cachuchua, 2004

fronted with an immense rock overhang: La Cachuchua. Yes, you have to drive under it, and no, the truck won't get stuck. The overhang protrudes straight out from the sheer cliff. This is where the high country begins. The air is already cooler, you can smell the oaks and pines, and butterflies flit from flower to flower.

The cliff is sheer, and it is here that *Agave potrerana,* the red-flowered agave, begins its range. *Agave potrerana* is abundant at higher elevations in the Carmens. The next closest population is in Chihuahua, and here in the Maderas is the only location in Coahuila where it has been recorded. This agave is another of those species that makes a person wonder how it came to be here and in abundant numbers. The plant is a medium-sized rosette—not as large as Havard's agave or slim-footed maguey—and medium green in color with a shallow root system. These agave cling precariously to the cliff face with roots anchored in small crevices. Farther up the mountain they are more abundant, but always in very rocky areas and most of the time on cliffs. The shaggy flowers remind me of an over-sized lechuguilla bloom. Hummingbirds, ants, bees, and orioles swarm the blooms for their sweet nectar.

One day a couple of summers ago we were exploring the nooks and crannies in the lower reaches of the cliff looking for wood rat nests, when Jonás called to Feliciano and me to come see what he had found. In a small sheltered crack in the cliff face were the remains of several candles and Mexican coins. Offerings had been placed there for a safe trip up and down the narrow mountain road. Perhaps the offerings had been placed there by miners or the loggers when they were cutting timber in the high country. These are small reminders of the people who were here before us—and they didn't have four-wheel drive! According to Jesús Maria Ramón and his brother Jorge Ramón, who spent much time here in years past when their father owned the Rancho Pilares, the loggers used burros to pull vehicles up the steep grades. I can only imag-

Candles and coins left as offerings, La Cachuchua. Photo J. D. Villalobos, 2004

ine the wrecks and close calls they must have experienced. Once several years ago, after a particularly heavy rain storm in late afternoon, the crews working on the mountain had to walk down part of the way, as they couldn't get a four-wheeler down La Cachuchua. One slide on ice or in mud in the wrong direction and truck and passengers end up at the bottom of the canyon.

La Cachuchua is a landmark on the mountain; the overhang is so enormous that underneath it the soil is very dry, hardly ever getting wet, even during storms. We have often stopped and sought shelter under the overhang during rainstorms. It is also a great place to stop, have a cup of coffee, and admire the view of the desert below. Animals use this spot for shelter and many times we have observed fresh bear tracks under the overhang. Mexican wood rats have nests in the many crevices and overhangs, and during the warmer months we see spiny crevice lizards sunning on the rocks.

I always look forward to seeing La Cachuchua, but always heave a sigh of relief when I am past it going up the mountain, and the sigh is even gustier when I have made the curve and reached the bottom of the grade on the way down the mountain. A friend visiting the Carmens said that everyone should be issued a shot of tequila before going up to meet La Cachuchua and another one before the equally hair-raising return trip.

I had heard of the Hacienda Piedra Blanca many times while living in West Texas, but I didn't know exactly where it was on the east side of the Carmen Mountains. In the mid-1990s, when Chabela Sellers and I were conducting a bird project on her ranch, La Escondida, in the Serranías del Burro, we drove down the long Valle de los Venados coming from La Linda. We speculated many times exactly where the old Hacienda Piedra Blanca was, and one day we pinpointed the location. She knew the general location as she lives nearby, so we started up the road that led toward the big cottonwood trees we could see from Ejido Morelos, which we believed had to be the Hacienda Piedra Blanca. We didn't get very far as the road was washed out, rough, and full of rocks. We didn't have four-wheel drive, so we turned around to plan for another day.

Many years ago ranchers on both sides of the border worked in this area. The grasslands were strong and there was abundant water. The late Hallie Stillwell, our neighbor on the Black Gap boundary, told Bill and I that the Stillwell family ranched Piedra Blanca for a number of years. They received a land grant from General Gerónimo Treviño in the late 1800s and the Stillwells moved their cattle to Coahuila. They crossed the Rio Grande at the well-known Stillwell Crossing located on the Adams Ranch. Years later the Stillwells had to discontinue ranching operations in Mexico and return to West Texas. Later a prominent Del Rio family owned the ranch. Seven different ranches, all located some distance away, used the water from the Piedra Blanca. When the communal land system program was established in Mexico, many of the large ranches were taken from landowners and became part of the ejido communal property system. Ejido residents generally made their living off the land, so the former grasslands became overused by too much grazing, resulting in loss of seed banks in some areas and regeneration of brush species in other areas. Wildlife numbers also continued to rapidly decrease, as hunting was a way of life and conducted on a year-round basis.

Hacienda Piedra Blanca, 2006

Many hectares of former grasslands are still here, but with rest they will return. Then perhaps the pronghorn can be reintroduced into this valley, which probably supported not only the pronghorn, but buffalo and mule deer in times past. We know that Mexican lobos were in this area, and perhaps one day when prey is abundant they too will be seen in the grasslands.

Once we moved to Coahuila and I became familiar with the mountain, I learned Piedra Blanca's precise location. During every trip to El Club, we passed the road to the main house where cottonwoods still stand. I could imagine shade under the trees, water bubbling up from a spring nearby, voices of the past in the wind.

CEMEX purchased the Hacienda Piedra Blanca, as it is recorded on the deeds. I was ecstatic. Hugo, Jonás, and I packed a lunch, cameras, and everything else we might need and headed out early one summer morning. It was hot early that day and with the dirt road up the Cuesta Malena under construction, the dust was so thick it rolled up over the hood of the truck like water. We turned north at El Melón and headed to the Valle de los Venados; the drive seemed longer than usual but at last we reached the turnoff. We followed Bill's directions—there are many little side roads, courtesy of the ejidos. We made a couple of turns and arrived at the gate. The cottonwoods were looming and I could see part of the old house. I am nearly as passionate about old houses as I am about working with wildlife. I couldn't wait to see this old hacienda. I knew it wasn't large; Bill had been here a couple of weeks ago and said, "Well, the house is not much, more an old rock and adobe shell." The entire area was overgrown with weeds that were head high in some places, and the old house was in a sad state of disrepair. But I wasn't disappointed. I could well imagine how it was years ago, the house gracious with fires in the fireplaces, lamplight, coffee on the stove, the wind in the trees. We explored the house, and decided that it could be repaired; this was a part of history and well worth saving.

Next, we could hear water trickling near the house but the weeds obscured the spring's loca-

Remains of adobe building at Hacienda Piedra Blanca, 2006

tion. We walked down to the old spring house, which still had a tin cup hanging on a wire outside. Leopard frogs were swimming merrily in the clear water. Huge pecan trees and the remains of an adobe building surrounded the spring area and large grassy areas were shaded by the trees. Grasslands, water, and wildlife would return to the lush diversity and abundance of the past. In the meantime, this area was a mecca for birds, as huge trees, native brush, water, and food sources were here for them. I could well imagine the many bird songs early in the morning. The former grasslands, once restored, would be important for sparrows, and burrowing owls, and serve as hunting grounds for raptors, loggerhead shrikes, and a host of other species. Shallow watering areas could be developed for birds to use for drinking and bathing in hot weather. The huge trees were potential nesting sites for black hawks, Swainson's hawks, and multiple species of songbirds. We heard Bell's vireo, blue grosbeak, painted buntings, varied buntings, black-throated sparrows, ash-throated flycatchers, and yellow-breasted chats in the nearby brush.

During the winter months when we were on our way to El Club we had observed a host of bird species using these overgrazed grasslands. Chipping, clay-colored, Brewer's, Lincoln's, and white-crowned sparrows; both mountain and western bluebirds; western meadowlarks; and huge flocks of lark buntings were all common. Nest boxes could be installed for cavity nesting species such as ash-throated flycatchers, elf owls, and bluebirds. The potential was here.

Looking out across the valley, my mind's eye brought to me vistas populated with pronghorn and mule deer increasing to levels of stability. On a cold winter night in the future, perhaps someone inside the house at Piedra Blanca will hear the lobo howl. Protection, good management, and a lot of hard work will make the dream real in time. I had finally seen Piedra Blanca, and I was filled with hope and delight.

19 Cañón el Álamo

History, species diversity, legends, ghosts, mines, rare cactus, and beautiful scenery all combine in a large canyon complex at the southern end of the Carmens. This canyon's original name was El Álamo on the old maps; recently local inhabitants call it Cañón San Isidro, probably because a ranch by this name was located in the canyon. Our home is called Casa San Isidro, also taken from the ranch name. Cañón Juárez is actually part of Cañón el Álamo, and Cañón Fronteriza is a large side canyon that joins Álamo. El Álamo begins high in the Cañón Temblores area, winds downward through Juárez, and then passes Fronteriza as it widens and snakes down the canyon. The canyon expands and narrows, still snaking downward, as it reaches the mouth, twisting through sheer limestone cliffs and out onto the desert floor. Here it disappears into a brushy arroyo, cutting into the loamy sand of the desert. Finally it ends, miles out in the desert joining the Jaboncillos Arroyo that eventually leads to Boquillas del Carmen.

Cañón el Álamo is one of the largest drainages on the west side of the Carmens. During the monsoon rains in summer and fall, this canyon, hurls immense quantities of water through the canyon crashing over boulders, moving trees, rearranging the landscape, and pouring out onto the hot desert. The arroyo is a sight to behold when all its fury is unleashed and water is roiling down the canyon. During heavy rains, the creek roars for several days and then the level begins to drop. From a muddy brown hue, filled with rocks, sticks, limbs, plants, and boulders, the water changes to a crystal-clear mountain stream sighing softly as it flows over the gravel-filled creek bed, shimmering like a million rhinestones in the early morning light. Flowers bloom, bobbing their heads over the sparkling waters.

For me, this is a joyful cycle. Late at night from our patio at Casa San Isidro I marvel at the light show of a furious thunderstorm, as I drink coffee and wait, knowing that the rains which fell for hours in the high country will run down the canyons and crevices and plummet down in newly created waterfalls. I don't have long to wait; I can hear from up-canyon a steady roar, getting closer and louder as it rounds the bend above our house and pushes through the willows, laying them flat as matchsticks, and then over the small dam and downward into a long pool, and then another small dam, crashing down over rocks and boulders, filling the deep tinajas, and clearing the creek of debris.

It is a sight to behold when Mother Nature is exuberant. I have watched the water swirl past, standing above the creek with a flashlight. The next morning the small dams aren't visible, the creek is higher, over ten feet deep, and no one will travel in the canyon until the floodwaters have abated somewhat. On the second morning, we are able to cross in low-gear four-wheel drive; the creek is still running bank to bank, but slower.

By late afternoon, the water is more docile, but still deep. The air is thick and heavy, and clouds are building in the north. Late that night I hear the thunder, and in the early morning hours the creek wakes me, roaring past the house. Gone is the docile stream, as I hear the boulders grating against each other rolling down the creekbed. The force of the water is moving them from the high country downward. I lay awake for several hours listening; dawn is close when I finally sleep. With coffee in hand, I move outside where I see the creek running fast and deep. The water is deceptively smooth on top, but beneath the surface a boiling mass takes everything in its path downstream. I enjoy my coffee and watch the birds around the house. There will be no crossing El Álamo today.

The birdlife of Cañón el Álamo is highly diversified, from the canyon mouth at the desert floor to the pine-oak habitat in the high country. There are many little niches and permanent water sources that draw birds to the area. Beginning at the lowest elevation in the canyon mouth, you leave the desert floor and enter the canyon. The sheer cliff walls are littered with overhangs and crevices that provide nesting sites for red-tailed and zone-tailed hawks. Canyon wrens perch on the cliff, sounding their familiar descending call, and white-throated swifts zig-zag in flight high above the cliff rim in the blue sky. In the canyon below, the brush along the arroyo provides many food sources and nesting sites. A few resident species are black-throated sparrow, black-tailed gnatcatcher, canyon towhee, northern mockingbird, greater roadrunner, phainopepla, scaled quail, mourning dove, rufous-crowned sparrow, northern cardinal, and pyrrhuloxia.

In spring and summer from the canyon mouth to the Casa San Isidro, the banks of the arroyo and surrounding hillsides are alive with birds. Scott's oriole; blue and black-headed grosbeak; painted, varied, and indigo buntings; yellow-breasted chat; ash-throated flycatcher; western and Cassin's kingbird; orchard and hooded oriole; Inca; white-winged, white-tipped, mourning, and common ground dove; Mexican jay; black-chinned, broad-tailed, blue-throated, and magnificent hummingbirds; lesser goldfinch; house finch; gray vireo; Bell's vireo; western screech owls; common poor-will; Cooper's hawk; golden eagle; peregrine falcon; summer, hepatic and western tanagers; and black and Say's phoebe all find this habitat to their liking.

At Casa San Isidro where I live, the yard is landscaped with native plants; the flower beds are the only concession to non-natives. Lantanas, roses, and bougainvillea fill the long beds providing nectar sources for butterflies, insects, birds, and bats. Water is available in a large fountain on the outside patio and in many of the small tinajas in the arroyo. The surrounding canyons and mountain slopes provide nesting sites, cover, and a mixture of habitats. There is overlap in species

Arroyo del Álamo, 2006

here where habitats begin and end. The matorral habitat along the arroyo gives way to oak and pinyon pine, and, farther up the canyon, to more oaks, big-tooth maple, and ponderosa pine. Resident bird species at Casa San Isidro include canyon towhee, Audubon's oriole, house finch, rufous-crowned sparrow, Mexican jay, rock and canyon wren, Say's phoebe, northern mockingbird, black-throated sparrow, mourning and white-winged dove, Inca, white-tipped and common ground doves, greater roadrunner, northern cardinal, phainopepla, lesser goldfinch, black-crested titmouse, golden eagle, red-tailed and Cooper's hawk, western screech owl, and common poor-will.

Spring brings the neotropical migrants that spend the spring and summer raising their young and then traveling south in the fall. Species numbers double in the warmer weather with the addition of the orioles, buntings, swallows, chats, tanagers, and hummingbirds. Fall brings a slower pace, as the neotropicals migrate south and the first cold front brings in a few sparrows. Later in November and December, the winter visitors arrive and the patios and yard resound with the song of white-crowned sparrows. Red-naped and Williamson's sapsuckers frequent the trees, searching for insects. Yellow-rumped warblers, ruby-crowned kinglets, and large flocks of pine siskins feed daily on insects and seeds in the yard. The northern goshawk, a resident of the higher elevations, moves down to hunt during the winter. Peregrines hunt the canyon for unsuspecting songbirds and doves, and American kestrel num-

Casa San Isidro, 2006

bers double during the winter with an influx of birds from the north. Spotted and green-tailed towhees and American robins scratch in the underbrush while the resident titmice scold every creature that dares to approach the bird feeders.

Farther up the canyon, Mexican jays are the dominant species, and black-crested titmice, bushtits, acorn woodpeckers, Cooper's hawks, and canyon towhees are the resident species that are joined by many of the aforementioned species in spring and fall.

Cañón el Álamo was also overgrazed for many years by cattle, horses, and goats. It was also severely overhunted until most of the native game animals were depleted. Cañón Fronteriza was the site of mining activity for many years; the famous hunter Ben Lily reportedly lived in the Carmens and hunted on a daily basis for the miners at Fronteriza. Years ago this area likely supported a riparian galley forest of native cottonwoods from the head of the canyon to its mouth at the desert floor. This is evidenced by several relic cottonwoods that remain along the arroyo. The constant trampling of cattle and horses and the feeding pattern of goats prevented cottonwood regeneration. By replanting native sapling cottonwoods, the next generation may see a galley forest of native cottonwoods on the arroyo banks.

Several of the old-timers who lived here in the canyon are sources on its colorful history, legends, and ghost stories. Just inside the canyon mouth, you round a curve and see a large cave ahead, the Cueva Elvida. The story goes that for many years a woman and her two daughters lived here in the cave and tended their small herd of goats. Evidence of indigenous peoples is present in the many broken *metates* and grinding stones both inside and outside the cave. Broken arrowheads, flint shards, and charred soil here and elsewhere in the Carmens are all reminders that others lived here long before the ranchers and goat herders. The top of the cave is black with smoke from many campfires. Life in this cave had to be hard—hot in the summer and cold in the winter. Imagine the sky leaden, the wind howling, darkness approaching, and you are alone with two small children and your goats in a cave. According to the story, the daughters grew up in the cave and moved to Múzquiz, and were eventually followed by their mother.

Farther up the canyon are remains of small rock houses, built of stones from the nearby arroyo. Still farther up, there is a small graveyard, called a *campo santo*. The campo santo consists of thirteen or fourteen graves, all small rock mounds, one topped with a metal cross and the others a wooden cross. Most lack names. Who were the people buried here? Were they miners, vaqueros, women, and children? One of the men on our project crew said that his grandfather was buried here, but he could not identify which grave since he was very young at the time.

El Álamo is also famous for ghosts, especially a woman who walks the canyon at night. I have heard many stories from many different people about the ghosts of San Isidro. Once several years ago it was bitter cold and raining when Jonás and I were headed to Múzquiz to a meeting. At the top of the Cuesta Malena, we noticed an old man standing on the side of the road. We stopped and he asked us for a ride to Múzquiz. Naturally we asked him about the mountain and its wildlife and such. Presently he asked us where we lived. Jonás replied that he lived at Pilares and that I lived at Casa San Isidro. The man asked if I had seen the woman walking in the canyon at night, and said that everyone knew about her and many had seen her at night. I replied that I hadn't seen her.

Another time, Jonás, my friend Valer Austin from Arizona, and I were coming back from photographing the Cuesta Malena, and met a young couple on the road whose vehicle had broken down. We stopped since they had a baby and it was cold and windy. We gave them a ride to their *ranchito* on the west side of La Encantada. On the way, they asked where we lived. Again, Pilares and Casa San Isidro. The young man asked if I were afraid to live there, and I replied that I was not. He mentioned ghosts at the house and said that his dad had worked there once. His wife added that she and her husband had once intended to spend the evening there. Shortly after they went to bed, the bed rose off the floor. "That was enough for us," she said, and they fled in the middle of the night.

Another story comes from the workers who remodeled the house at Casa San Isidro before Bill and I moved in. When they dug the foundations for the patios that wrap around the front of the house, they discovered leg chains dating from the late eighteenth century when mines in this area were operating. According to regional lore, indigenous people employed in the mine were put in leg chains at night to prevent them from running away.

According to a story told by Don Beto, a legend himself and for years our cook at Pilares, a certain fellow robbed the bank many years ago in Múzquiz. He hightailed it from town to the Carmens and headed up Cañón el Álamo to Casa San Isidro. Reaching the house, he buried the gold he had stolen in the robbery in the floor of what is now the living room. Don Beto assured me the gold is buried under four rows of mosaic tile inside a long rectangle of plain saltillo tiles. If the gold is here, it will remain safely buried, at least during our tenure.

The first time I saw Casa San Isidro, it was basically a shell of a house and there were three goats standing inside the door. The yard contained small horse pens and a tin shack to hold horse feed and saddles. It was evident that the house had been in its "incomplete" state for many years. Everyone I have questioned about why the house was not completed tells the same story—the house is haunted. However, photos of the house in 1936 show that it consisted of the current living area and dining room. Apparently, the house began as a one-room affair, which was ex-

Cañón el Álamo, 2006

panded over the years by various tenants. CEMEX added several rooms and finished the house, while also building large covered patios on the front and side and a smaller sunny patio with a large fountain. The house is spacious and welcoming; we have entertained hundreds of people over the past ten years.

Does the house have ghosts? Well, yes, but they don't bother me. I am not a naturally superstitious person, and I have spent many nights in the canyon alone. I am a firm believer that there is an explanation for any noise in the night or unusual incident. However, there are several unexplained phenomena that I have noted. The first is beans cooking in the night. I woke up one night several years ago smelling beans cooking, and so I padded into the kitchen to check on the pot. The maid had not left any beans cooking. This fragrance is distinctive, there is no mistaking it. After that first time, I awakened in the middle of the night many times to the smell of beans cooking. I never said a word to my husband about these olfactory experiences, as he tends to brush off remarks of this sort as the product of my personal dreamland. About a year and a half ago he woke me up in the middle of the night, saying, "Do you have beans cooking? I can smell them." I replied, "Yes, it is the ghost of San Isidro, and she cooks beans a lot at night." He promptly got up and went to the kitchen, and returned to the bedroom saying, "Well, there are no beans cooking, but I sure smell them!" My friend Valer Austin has also smelled beans cooking in the wee hours at Casa

San Isidro. Other people experiencing the same cookery in the night add validity to my own ghost story.

Another unexplained phenomenon at Casa San Isidro took place in December 2005. One night I heard a loud crash, but I didn't get up to investigate because the wind was blowing and I figured one of the pots on the patio had blown over. The next morning, the maid Lupita was standing in the middle of the kitchen glaring at a large rock. I asked her where it came from. She said, "I don't know. Did you put it here? What is it for?" I replied, "I didn't put it there—why would I put a big rock in the middle of the kitchen floor?" We threw it in the arroyo and wrote it off to the ghost of San Isidro. The house is constructed of rock, the kitchen walls are brick, but no rocks were missing from the walls. Where did it come from?

Yet another inexplicable incident occurred in winter as well. I was sitting at the end of the dining room table working on my computer. I heard the doorknob turn and looked up in surprise. I was at home alone, as Lupita and her husband had gone home for the night and Bill was in Del Rio. I hadn't heard anyone drive up. I walked over and opened the door, and found nothing and no one. I figured it was the wind. I went back to the computer and in just a few minutes the door handle turned again. This time I just stared at the door. Admittedly, I was a little creeped out: there was no wind and I didn't hear the screen door open. I watched in amazement as the door knob turned rapidly several times. By then I had goose bumps, but I was determined to find an explanation. I jerked open the door, and once again, nothing.

Finally, at another time of apparent ghostly activity in the house, I was alone at San Isidro, and it was summer. The windows were open, and it was hot with very little breeze. I went to bed late, and several hours later a noise woke me and my dog Cappy ran into the living room barking. I assumed there was a bear outside prowling around, and so I went through the living room and opened the side door from the dining room to the patio, but nothing was amiss. I went back to bed thinking that the bear or whatever animal it was had left. I woke the next morning and went into the kitchen to make my coffee. All the doors were open in the two glass-fronted hutches filled with dishes in the dining room, and so were the doors in a glass-fronted bookcase in a bedroom. Again, I have no explanation for this incident nor for the others. Perhaps the house does have ghosts, but they appear to be friendly; they don't bother me and I am no threat to them. I have not seen nor heard the woman that walks the canyon at night, but I do wish the woman who cooks the beans at night would change her menu to early morning coffee.

In truth, I love being alone in the canyon, as it is a peaceful place. Wildlife numbers are coming back, and in the spring, summer, and fall, the canyon is a bear highway. The canyon is a source of many different foods for the bears and a main access route from the mid elevations to the higher country. One morning in early spring, I looked out the dining room window and nine elk cows were grazing on the grass along the creek bank. Gray foxes, ringtails, bobcats, Carmen Mountain white-tailed deer, javelina, puma, black bears, and a host of small mammals and birds all call this canyon home. We share it with them and enjoy the solitude the canyon offers.

After the abuse of countless years of grazing, the land in Cañón el Álamo is making a rapid comeback after nine years of rest from domestic livestock. Native grasses are now on the hillsides, sapling oaks and junipers grow on the mountainsides, and the creek is no longer trampled and polluted. Five years ago you could see bare ground in many areas on the mountainside; these patches are now covered with native vegetation, vines, grasses, and wildflowers. The only problem is the encroachment of brush species such as uña de gato and whitebrush. Both are by-products of overgrazing, and both are so thick in some areas that they have formed impenetrable thickets. The elk favor this canyon much of the year and are proving to be a good management tool because they browse the brush species. As for humans trekking through the canyon, currently I am the only living woman who does so and I haven't taken to walking the canyon at night.

The Cuesta Malena is the unofficial southern landmark that heralds the beginning of the western side of the Carmen Mountains. In Mexico, a *cuesta* usually refers to an area at the top of a hill or a pass in the mountains. In the past, the Malena was called the Cuesta Plomo, and then its name was changed to honor a local woman upon her death. Malena, who lived with her husband at the foot of the winding road up the Cuesta, had a restaurant in a small adobe building. Reportedly she was a great cook and was respected and well-liked by the local residents. Her grave stands alone on the roadside at the bottom of Cuesta Malena. I try and remember to take flowers to her grave on special occasions like Christmas and the Day of the Dead. Her grave is surrounded by a sagging barbed wire fence, marked with a cross on a mound of dirt and stones. Some people say her husband is buried beside her, but I see no evidence of a second grave. Her tomb is in a lonely little spot, and the flowers I take brighten the grave site and let her know that she is remembered. One year someone else remembered her at Christmas with fresh flowers. She is one of the many residents whom I would have liked to have known.

The Cuesta itself is a natural wonder, comprised of a towering series of white sandstone pillars that look surreal. There are no other rock formations in the area that even remotely resemble these. Perhaps they are sentinels that guard the entrance to the west side of the Carmens. This sandstone formation appears to be an afterthought, as if the world maker had some sandstone left over, and being weary after eons of arranging the continental plates and weather systems that created the mountains, decided to plunk it down here in a number of separate piles. It is marvelous to behold in the early morning light or at sunset.

I had heard of the Cuesta Malena and knew the location from maps. The first time I saw it I was literally stunned by the rock formations, as well as the large statue of Jesus that someone had placed atop the huge rounded boulder at the base of the pillars. It was late October 2000, a year before we moved to Coahuila. I had planned on joining Billy Pat in the Carmens for a couple of days. We normally crossed at Boquillas in the famous boat *La Enchilada*. The day before when I arrived at the Rio Grande crossing about 9:00 a.m., Bill was to meet me on the other side with the truck. On reaching the small parking lot in Big Bend National Park, I found the area swarming with U.S. Customs, Border Patrol agents, and park service officials. I was told it was impossible to cross, as it had been closed due to a drug bust. I asked if I could go down to the river bank and yell across to my husband who was meeting me. First they said no, and then finally changed their mind. I walked down, escorted by a customs agent. He left and I waited about fifteen minutes for Bill to arrive. We had a yelling contest across the river, and then he left and I

headed home. Several phone calls later it was decided that I would drive to Del Rio early the next morning and there I would meet someone to drive me to the Carmens.

I left early, met the driver, and in late afternoon we were heading up toward the Cuesta Malena. A storm was rolling in and the fog was low on the ground and swirling over the top of the Cuesta. We rounded a sharp turn in the road and were confronted by towering pillars. The pillars literally rake the sky, and the boulder with the statue at the bottom seems to fit this natural splendor. The image stayed with me all the way down the other side to Pilares.

The Cuesta is one of my favorite places. I always marvel at the austere beauty of the pillars, and the native wildflowers and oaks growing below the pillars make the area seem like a giant native garden with natural statues carved in haphazard fashion. Any and all approaching storms shroud the Cuesta Malena in clouds so thick that visibility is almost zero. Often the sky at Los Pilares in early morning is clear, while directly to the east a heavy, dark cloud bank covers the Cuesta. Many times we have been reduced to creeping along at five miles an hour going up and through the Cuesta, only to suddenly emerge in bright sunshine on the other side. The Cuesta Malena also serves as a natural pass between the Carmens and the western portion of the Sierra Encantada.

Cuesta Malena, 2002

21 Campo Dos

Campo Dos, the highest camp in the Carmens, is well hidden in a narrow portion of Cañón el Oso. Leaving Campo Cinco, the road twists and turns gradually climbing upward. This road provides an experiential lesson in plant habitat. All it takes is a few feet of elevation difference: going down a few feet you enter the oaks, and then uphill a few feet, you are back in fir and pine, followed by another descent to the oaks. This pattern continues for several miles.

The rhyolite cliffs tower toward the heavens and the slopes are very steep. Peregrine falcons, northern goshawks, and zone-tailed and Cooper's hawks are all here, protected in their high-mountain sanctuary. Along the road you see evidence of past logging operations. The loggers cut untold numbers of Douglas and Coahuila fir, as well as pine and oak, but the firs took the biggest hit. Huge stumps remain as well as whole trees that were felled and left to rot. The tree trunks and stumps are silver with age.

Farther up the mountain, a road turns to the left, which goes to the highest peak in the Carmens, Pico Loomis, at an elevation of over twenty-seven hundred meters. This road always requires a four-wheeler and progress is slow. The road snakes upward toward the peak, the canopy overhead is close, you occasionally see tiny patches of blue sky, and firs are dominant with oaks scattered about. Finally you reach the sum-

Cliffs on road to Campo Dos, 2003

mit and the view is extraordinary. Pico Loomis is higher than the mountains north in Texas, and higher than the adjacent mountains in Coahuila. Looking south, you see the links in the chain that connect the Mexican mountains; far south the Santa Rosas join the Encantada, where they in turn join the Carmens at the pass in the Cuesta Malena. The Carmens stretch north, joining Big Bend National Park on the east boundary and the west boundary of the Black Gap Wildlife Management Area at the old Adams Ranch. The Carmens stretch even farther, almost to the Santiago range in West Texas. I have been to Pico Loomis many times; this is one spot where I never tire of looking at the view. Shadows, sunsets, storms, clouds, dust, rain, and sunrise change the mountains' appearance dramatically. Once I took my cell phone to Pico Loomis and called to make an airline reservation for a trip home to Virginia. I bet the woman who booked my reservation wouldn't have believed that the phone call came from high on a mountain in northern Coahuila, Mexico.

This is but one of the many areas along the road to Campo Dos that offer breathtaking views, a remarkable diversity of flora and fauna, and the wildness of the vertiginous mountain vistas. As far as the eye can see, there is one mountain after another, whereas small mountains surrounded by desert far below appear to be tiny hills from my lofty vantage point.

Heading on up the road to Campo Dos, a less traveled road veers to the left and is locally referred to as Hummingbird Canyon, through the old-timers call it Campo Coyote. This road climbs steadily upward for about a mile, passing a spring-fed marshy area. Wildflowers bloom along the old roadside, and remains of an Indian camp are evidenced by flint chippings. Farther on you break out of the forest onto the top of a cliff. Here is another grand view—below is Cañón Frijoles where oaks predominate in the foothills and pines and fir in the higher elevations. Miles below on the desert floor, heat waves rise, creating mirages. On the top of the cliff, the wind is brisk, bringing the scent of pine and oaks. Clouds are building far to the south behind the peaks of the Sierra Santa Fé del Pino; perhaps rain is in the forecast.

Farther up the narrow canyon road, you round a bend and across the valley to the east the Serranías del Burro shimmer blue and purple in the distance. Close by, the cliffs of Cañón Escondido rise skyward, and below the canopy of pines and oaks cover the trail going down Cañón el Oso.

Still we head upward and then finally after a hairpin turn, we move down into a canyon. Water is abundant at this high elevation: small springs seep out of the banks along the roadside, and a mountain brook tumbles over rocks, making mini-waterfalls. Finally, one last hill and cross the creek, and you are at Campo Dos.

The camp is located in a narrow portion of the canyon. The old logging road went behind the camp, while the new road is at the right of and above the creek. The creek rushes noisily over the rocks, and the water is clear and ice cold. Currently there are three cabins—a cook cabin and two cabins with baths are placed side by side on a slight rise.

The camp is comfortable. We stay here when we are working in the high country. Early morning, even in summer, the temperature is in the forties and fifties. By late August, the temperature drops even lower during the night, and early mornings are very cool until the sunshine comes over the high peaks and down into the canyon. Coffee by the outside fire pit is a pleasure. Once the sun is over the peaks, the camp comes alive with birdsong. Painted redstarts, Mexican jays, bushtits, titmice, yellow-eyed juncos, and acorn woodpeckers all seem to compete for the best songster title. By the creek, butterflies flitter over the water and along the muddy edges. Several Carmen Mountain white-tailed deer amble down to the creek for a morning drink, paying not the slightest attention to us.

In July and August, the mountain shows off her colors with multitudes of wildflowers of red, yellow, blue, violet, white, orange, pink, magenta, and all hues in between. Bees, butterflies, and birds all take nectar from the many species of flowers. The wild roses along the roadside and creek bank have small pink blooms. Campo Dos in summer is a great place to observe wildflowers, birds, and butterflies. In July we stop along the road to pick blackberries tart and refreshing.

On May 7, 2003, Feliciano, Jonás, Santi, and I had hauled our field equipment and camp supplies to Dos for five days of bat netting. We set up camp and then headed down the creek to arrange our mist nets over wide pools of slow-moving water. We furled the nets and headed back to camp. I took one cabin, the guys the other. Pulling on a sweater by late afternoon, I knew that we would have been sweltering in the desert heat in the lower elevations, yet here I needed a sweater to ward off the chill. The canyon cools off rapidly once the sun sets behind the high cliffs.

We cooked dinner, cleaned up the kitchen, and by dusk we were in place along the creek

Longspur columbine at Campo Dos, 2003

with our data-collecting station positioned on the tail-gate of the truck. We weren't disappointed; right at dark the bats started flying. We could hear hoary bats hitting the nets and emitting their nasal vocalizations as well as chewing holes in the nets. We put on our headlamps and headed down to the creek. Taking bats out of the nets was steady work, and we caught forty-two, including big brown bats, northern long-eared myotis, hoary bats, Townsend's big-eared bats, a myotis species, western small-footed myotis, pocketed free-tailed bats, and a beautiful northern saw-whet owl and several whip-poor-wills. At 2:00 a.m. we were freezing and the bats had ended their nighttime flight—perhaps they were feeling the cold also. We furled the nets and headed back to the cabins. We made *café con leche*, which is a lot of hot milk with a little coffee and sugar. Delicious; I took the last cup with me to my cabin. We took the seats off the four-wheelers to prevent the bears from chewing them up, and called it a night.

My cabin was cold; I snuggled down in my sleeping bag and wrote journal notes and finished my coffee. Then lights out. It was warm in my sleeping bag and in minutes I was lulled asleep by the sound of the creek right below my window and the whip-poor-wills calling.

The next day we prepared specimens and field notes. We ran the small mammal lines, which are galvanized live traps in a line, each spaced at a certain distance and baited. In addition we set up herp arrays, which are "Y"-shaped tin about eighteen inches high and thirty feet long; at the end of each line of the "Y," a bucket is recessed in the ground. Small snakes and lizards and some small mammals follow the line of tin since it obstructs their path, and upon reaching the end, they drop into the bucket. We were ready for bat netting at dusk.

It was another good night for bats, as we caught forty-nine. There were no new species that second night, except for pallid bats, which I was surprised to find at this elevation. By 2:00 a.m. we were freezing yet again, even wrapped up in Mexican woolen blankets and perched on the rocks along the creek. It was quiet in the canyon and inky black. Suddenly, we all heard it—a tree loudly creaking in the wind. The whip-poor-wills and owls immediately quit calling. It seemed that all the critters were waiting to see what the tree was going to do next: fall over or continue to creak in the wind. Shortly the eastern and western screech owls began calling again, the whip-poor-wills joined in, and I breathed a sigh of relief. Dark as it was, if the tree had fallen we would have had no idea which direction to move away from it.

Sleepy and cold, we headed back to camp and to our cabins. The next day we spent with the usual camp chores, field notes, running mammal and herp lines, and preparing specimens. We moved the nets a little farther down the creek since we were catching many repeats in the current location. We had color-banded the many hoary and big brown bats that we were constantly recapturing. Just several hundred yards down

Mountain stream at Campo Dos, 2003

the creek, we were catching more bats than we could weigh and measure. The first flight found us busy, bats were flying everywhere, and this lasted until midnight. We furled the nets at one point until we could catch up on data collection. One big surprise was a western yellow bat, which was our first record of this species in the Carmens. We also netted two very small myotis that would take further work to identify. We color-marked the hoary bats and the big brown bats in this area to see if we would get repeats the following evening.

The next night the wind picked up; we drank *café con leche* and waited, shivering in our blankets. The bats weren't flying, so at midnight we furled the nets and headed to camp. The wind was blowing cold from the north; we made fresh coffee, had late-night tacos, and headed to our cabins. I snuggled down in my sleeping bag, prepared to go to sleep early, and suddenly I felt movement on my foot. It took me about two seconds to evacuate the sleeping bag and locate the culprit—a deer mouse. After removing the mouse from my bedding, I went back to bed and had just fallen asleep when this persistent mouse, or perhaps it was another one, decided to visit again. This time it was in my hair, so again I leapt out of the bag to chase the mouse. This scenario ran another three times before the mouse finally gave up. I was wide awake now. I snuggled down getting warm and listening to the wind in the pines and the creek below my window, and hopeful that the mouse was sufficiently terrorized by the giant chasing him that he gave up and sought a warm spot elsewhere. Probably in my boot.

Three of us were back at Campo Dos for another five days of bat netting in August—this time Feliciano, Jonás, and me. We arrived mid-afternoon at Dos and unloaded our equipment and set up camp. It was cool and the air crisp, with a bright blue sky and not a cloud in sight. We set out mammal traps in Campo Coyote, put up the mist nets along the creek below Campo Dos, and cooked dinner. I always cook dinner the first night, and then the guys take over the cooking on subsequent evenings, and we all clean up. Dusk found us at the creek waiting on the first flight of bats. It was cold, even in heavy jackets, stocking hats, and woolen blankets. We waited and waited in the cold and caught only one hoary bat and then a single eastern red bat, marking the first record of this species in the Carmens. The eastern red was worth the wait! On the following day, the wind blew throughout and it rained and continued to rain the rest of the week. After two days in the rain, we gave it up and headed back down the mountain.

Campo Dos in the spring and summer is a great place to work, but in the fall and winter it is downright frigid. Storms blow in over the high peaks, and ice and snow are more frequent here than in the lower canyons and foothills.

In late November 2002, several Mexican biologists were staying with us working in the Carmens, along with Matthew Tyrell from the University of Arkansas who was doing fieldwork on the history of wildfire occurrences on the mountain. The day before we had had a big Thanksgiving dinner at Casa San Isidro. Our son Matt was home on leave from the Marines, so I cooked a traditional Thanksgiving dinner and invited the Carmen biologists and the visiting researchers. In spite of the cold temperatures and dark skies we had a great dinner, and we celebrated long into the night. The next morning it was cold with an icy mist and wind. Bill and Matt headed back to the Texas border where Matt had to pick up his vehicle and head back to North Carolina. I drove to Pilares to pick up the visiting researchers and Jonás for a trip up to the high country so that they could complete some fieldwork before they left the next day. The weather was getting colder, and the mist turned to sleet about halfway up the mountain. Jonás and I dropped off the visitors at Campo Cinco to take their samples and we headed up to Campo Dos to collect mammal traps that we had left at the camp cook house.

The weather was bitter cold, the wind was howling, and the clouds were boiling over the mountain tops. We reached Campo Dos well past lunchtime. We hastily made a quick cup of coffee to warm up and then gathered the traps. Standing on the porch, I marveled at the storm. The clouds were a low swirling mass, like ghostly fingers swirling along at ground level; the trees were moaning and groaning in the wind, the force of the wind bending the pines and firs; branches were creaking; the sleet was coming down steady with a few snowflakes. The mountain gods were wreaking havoc. The forces of nature never cease to amaze me—Campo Dos was enclosed in a cocoon of clouds and visibility was practically zero. The wind would die down to complete silence one minute and the next you could hear the wind high up in the ridges and then closer, roaring down the canyon. The trees would shudder and bend, sometimes almost double. The fury of the storm has been witnessed in this canyon many times, and I was awed by the raw beauty of the elements all coming together at once. 'Twas a wild dance of nature, the melding of pent-up forces, primeval. I will always remember that storm as Mother Nature on a truly exhilarating rampage.

22 Cañón Moreno

Many of the canyons in the Carmens are tucked away in the mountain, hidden from view. Until you are very familiar with this mountain chain, it is not evident just how much country is here, and how the many canyons and mountains are assembled. Moreno is one such canyon. I have been to Moreno many times over the last nine years, and yet I never tire of it.

Cañón Moreno is one of the well-kept secrets of the mountain; there is no roadway for vehicles. Once there was a road of sorts but with time it has faded to a trail that heads up the mountain to intersect with Cañón Carboneras. Traveling up Cañón el Álamo into the Juárez area, you come to a couple of forks in the road. The first goes right and up toward the Mesa de los Fresnos and the second goes straight by the old casa and up the canyon. Soon the canyon ends, and off to the right Cañón Temblores begins. Across the creek and to the left there is a faintly marked trail. Crossing the boulder-strewn arroyo you start walking along the left bank of the creek winding through the oaks and pines.

The air is hot and close in the confines of this narrow passage up the canyon. Breathing deeply, you smell the hot scent of pine and a gentle puff of wind rustles the oak leaves. Taking care, I always watch along this part of the trail: northern black-tailed rattlesnakes are fairly common in the area. They blend in well with the leaf litter, grasses, and weeds, and it is always a breath-catching moment when

Black-tailed rattlesnake, Cañón Moreno.
Photo J. D. Villalobos, 2005

you hear that warning rattle. Sometimes you see them before they rattle, coiled up in the trail or off to the side under a rock ledge. Farther on the canyon widens and you start seeing the first of many pools of water that you will encounter for quite a distance up the canyon. The trail winds along the creek; the pools are quiet here. The water is clear as crystal and not as cold as the high mountain pools.

Farther on, the trail begins a steady climb to the high country. The air is cooler, and oaks and grama and muhly grasses make small park-like areas. There is a spring where the water flows year-round, and since cattle and horses have been removed the native cottonwoods are finally beginning the regeneration process evidenced by saplings springing up. The remains of an old corral and water trough are in a clearing about midway up the mountain. Vaqueros camped here and used the corrals to pen their horses and cattle when grazing them in the high country. Black bears love this canyon; there are many oaks with acorns in the fall, the slopes below the summits have many overhangs and cliffs that bears can use for hibernation sites. In early spring the grasses, Wright's tick clover, and Mexican conopholis provide food for bears emerging from hibernation.

Climbing ever upward, twisting and winding around the mountain on a late spring or early summer day, you marvel at the wildflowers, the many species of oaks, the dark green of pines against the blue sky, plains prickly pear cactus with yellow flowers, weeping juniper, and pinyon pine. Long-petal echeverias are common—light green rosettes with tiny bloom stalks topped with orange-red flowers that grow among the rocks. These succulents form small rock gardens, their roots firmly entrenched in crevices and cracks in the rocks. The trail gets steep in some places, and then levels out for a short distance. You climb steadily upward, and finally reach the summit of the canyon at Carboneras.

One of the most beautiful canyons in the Maderas, Moreno begins in a park-like setting of

Pools in Cañón Moreno, 2005

dant bear sign in the canyon. Beto Martinez had hiked in the canyon that morning to check the snare while we were checking barrel traps in other areas. At about 10:00 a.m. he called on the radio saying that we had a big bear caught in the snare and that it was uncollared. Jonás radioed back to Beto that we were on the way, and Hugo called in to say that he was nearby in Temblores checking elk and would meet us to help with the bear. The three of us arrived at about the same time, and Beto met us at the beginning of the trail; we separated our equipment and distributed it in our backpacks and headed up the canyon.

oaks and native grasses and ends high in the mountain in a pine-oak association. The many pools and tinajas in the arroyo are magical places; birds, reptiles and amphibians, and the native wildlife all depend on these water sources. The clear pools of unpolluted water gently flow downward, going underground in some places and then springing back to the surface farther downstream.

In June 2005 it was sweltering hot, and we were capturing and radio-collaring bears and had set black bear leg-hold snares in the canyon. Lugging a heavy barrel trap into this area was not possible; snares were easy and there was abun-

Elk in Cañón Moreno, 2005

Almost immediately we saw a black-tailed rattlesnake, but we didn't have time to worry about him. We needed to get to the bear since it was getting hot in the canyon. We huffed up the last hill where the trap site was located above the creek on a slope. The bear was fat and in excellent shape. Judging from size, it looked like a male, and definitely not happy. Popping teeth and huffing were indications of just how ticked off this bear was. Were we surprised once we got the bear immobilized and began the work-up—the bear was a very large female and based on size and teeth, probably an older female. She is the largest female we have caught in the Carmens. We worked her up quickly, taking measurements, data, samples, and putting on her radio collar. The immobilizing drug lasts about forty-five minutes to an hour; the bear wakes up slowly and is disoriented for a short time. The four of us hefted her up and moved her to deeper shade, and packed up our equipment.

I have always made it a policy to stay with each bear to monitor respiration until she or he is fully recovered and able to walk away. This is good practice, particularly if you are working in an area with a large bear population. It prevents other bears from coming into the immediate area and perhaps fighting with the immobilized bear. In the case of a female with small cubs, adult males may kill the cubs when the sow is unable to protect her young.

Beto and Hugo headed back down the canyon to resume their daily activities and we moved down to the creek to wait for the sow to wake up and move away from the trap site. The temperature was climbing steadily, clouds were building up in the south, and the air was still. We waited in the shade, splashing our faces with the cool water. Shortly the bear began moving, and then slowly got to her feet and wandered up the canyon, no worse the wear for her ordeal. We named her Margarita. Radio-collared bears have radio frequency numbers as well as tiny microchips inserted under the skin of the shoulder blades, but for many purposes, having a name for each individual is useful.

Margarita proved to be quite a bear. She has one of the smallest home ranges of all the radio-collared black bears in our study site. Following radio telemetry over a period of time, we found she seldom moved very far. She had everything she needed in her mountain canyon. In June 2006 she had two cubs with her; we saw her once when she moved down into the lower reaches of the canyon searching for food. The tiny cubs were marching along behind her in single file. She was in good condition, fat, and jet black. When we received the evaluation of our age data we were surprised to see she was thirteen years old. She has been on this mountain a long time producing cubs. She is secretive, preferring the hidden mountain canyon; perhaps her secretive nature has been a factor in her survival for so many years.

Her den site was so deep in the rock and caves of the canyon that we couldn't get a radio signal from mid-December when she hibernated until she emerged from her den in mid to late April. I could well imagine her snug in her den with tiny cubs while the winds howled down the canyon, icy rain pelted the sierra, and time marched on until one warm spring day she led her cubs from the den into the outside world for the first time.

Even though she is old, her teeth are good, and she is in excellent physical condition. Perhaps she will live many more years in her mountain hideaway. She has seen the storms, heard the winds, watched flash floods come down the canyon, laid down panting in the shade on hot summer days, and gorged herself on acorns in the fall, and taken her cubs to the creek where they played and splashed in the water under her watchful eye. She has seen many moons and sunrises, and we can hope she has many more.

23 Cañón Morteros

Cañón Morteros lies on the southeast end of the project area marked by a rambling house perched on the top of a slope. Down below the Chihuahuan Desert stretches for miles. To the southwest is the Ejido San Miguel, and farther south the Sierra Santa Fé del Pino range; to the west the jagged peaks of the Sierra de Hechiceros rise behind the Sierra San Vicente. This is hot desert country, and Cañón Morteros is definitely a hot desert canyon. Directly east of the house the canyon mouth beckons, and high on the mountain, directly left of the road, you see a large, almost perfectly square hole in the cliff face. This natural opening appears to be literally carved into the rock. Many years ago indigenous people, possibly Jumano Indians, carried their dead to this cave for burial. How they managed to pack dead weight to the cave is beyond me. The slope is very steep, and each step is difficult. Hauling dead weight from the top of the cliff down to the cave would also be hazardous. Perhaps the terrain was different then and access to the cave was easier. I prefer to think they made the difficult trek up the mountain to carry their beloved dead to their final resting place.

The view from the cave is incredible, as it faces the southwest and is protected from the elements by the deep recess inside the opening. Broken metates and *manos* (grinding stones) litter the cave floor in the fine dirt. It appears that many bodies were stacked one on top of the other, separated by hand-woven lechuguilla and sotol mats. Remains of woven net-type bags and nearly petrified peyote remnants are also strewn about the cave. Perhaps the immediate area served as a seasonal camp when the *tunas* (prickly pear cactus fruits) were ripe, or maybe it was acorns or mesquite beans. Over the years the site has been disturbed by goats and people. A few tin cans are evidence of modern visitors. In 2005, an archaeology workshop was held at El Carmen for staff and biologists from the Sabinas area. The cultural resources agency for Coahuila State was made aware of the site and the cave is protected.

Farther inside the canyon and just above the arroyo that runs the length of the canyon is another Indian cave. This one is smaller, and was definitely used for everyday living. The ceiling of the cave is charred black from fires over many decades, and broken metates, manos, and many small chippings from arrowheads have been found inside or nearby. This cave was also used for a time for sheltering goats. One story about the canyon tells about a man who committed a crime in Múzquiz, and fled straight for the Carmens where he holed up in the canyon for a period of time, using the smaller cave as his hiding place.

Morteros is a very well-watered canyon; the spring in the upper reaches of the canyon is strong and supplies water via pipeline to the lower desert country as well as the house, and several *pilas* (above-ground water storage tanks) and

Burial cave in Cañón Morteros, 2004

troughs in the canyon proper. This canyon is one of the few areas on the west side of the Carmens where mescal bean grows.

Inside the canyon there are numerous buttes of creamy yellow, orange, and pinkish sandstone, a contrast to the dark volcanic rocks that comprise the mountains in the canyon. Vegetation is mixed with many invader species and encroachment by undesirable natives. This canyon is probably the most overgrazed on the west side of the Carmens. Thousands of goats were camped here for many years, and the result is a landscape dominated by prickly pear with few grasses and literally several thousand hectares of mariola and guayule. Beginning on the banks of the arroyo and reaching nearly to the top of the mountain, the stands of guayule and mariola are so dense they actually form a knee-high thicket, choking out native grasses and other vegetation. Both of these plants have rubber content and they also tend to hybridize. Neither is utilized by wildlife species. Native vegetation is better represented along the winding arroyo that runs the length of the canyon. Littleleaf leadtree, Havard's agave, evergreen sumac, Mexican pistachio, mescal bean, Mexican persimmon, and whitebrush all grow along the arroyo drawing on underground moisture.

The large arroyo is limestone, whereas the buttes are sandstone, and the mesas and mountain tops are volcanic, dark red to black. The arroyo also contains many fossils; you only have to walk along the gravely creek bed and spend a few minutes looking to discover numerous small fossils. Common fossils in this area are snails, turritellas, ammonites, calamitids, and various shells.

Near the end of the canyon, oaks and junipers appear along the arroyo. Black-capped vireos nest in this area during the summer months, along with a host of other songbirds. Cañón Morteros is an interesting place with many different rock formations, caves, mesas, buttes, the long arroyo, a burial site that looks like a tomb carved into the sheer cliff face, caves with remains of Indian camps, crystal-clear water from a mountain spring, and miles of brush vegetation. The canyon is nearly devoid of wildlife; bears use it traveling from one series of hills and small mountains to the next. A few javelina are resident and fewer deer. Both Carmen Mountain white-tails and mule deer are resident; the mule deer prefer the lower reaches of the canyon and the Carmen Mountain white-tails utilize the steep slopes and the higher end of the canyon. The landscape was altered dramatically by many decades of overgrazing. Domesticated animals, as well as the corrals, dipping vats, fenced pastures, and general trash from goat and cattle operations have all been removed. Water troughs and pilas have been made wildlife friendly. Time and aggressive management techniques are needed to begin the re-vegetation of native grasses, forbs, and shrubs. The canyon is being rested.

In the course of our fieldwork we have stumbled onto several graves with no markers. We found one on the road to Campo Uno, a slight hump of dirt covered with rocks. At the head of the grave, we scratched around in the soil and found the remains of a candle.

During the summer of 2006, Beto Martinez was walking across an area below the high country, a transition zone of yucca-sotol-grassland. In this particular area there is evidence of a large Indian camp, and a goat camp was located here for many years because of the nearby spring. After an afternoon rain shower, Beto was looking for tracks. As he moved away from the old camp site, he noticed something sticking up out of the sandy soil along a small wash. He investigated and there was a bone, obviously a human arm bone, sticking straight up out of the soil, minus the hand. He and Jonás investigated further late that afternoon. The next morning when I arrived at the office, they showed me a photo. Of course, we returned to the site to take coordinates, photograph the skeleton and the site, record the vegetation, and take measures to protect the site until a time when the Mexican authorities decide what to do with "Lobo Man," as I have dubbed the skeleton.

The grave appears to have been hastily dug, just deep enough to hold the body. There are no remnants of clothing; it seems that the person was buried *sin ropas* (without clothes). The skeleton is that of an adult, literally folded up into a fetal position, with one arm reaching skyward and the other tucked in around his/her knees. The skull had been fractured. Whatever happened, it was a violent death, a cold grave in a lonely spot, no marker on the grave, and no clothes, not even a blanket. Hopefully carbon dating will tell us at least the approximate date that the person was buried. I had an extra cotton blouse on the four-wheeler so we carefully covered the skeleton, replaced the dirt, and placed a rock marker on the burial spot. We will wait and see what the results reveal. I am torn between leaving the lonely grave intact and having the skeleton moved to a permanent exhibit. The skeleton is an important part of area history, and may give us information on at least one of the indigenous tribes that inhabited the area, age at death, and gender. Perhaps after the bones are carbon dated, they can be returned to the original grave site.

Several weeks before this discovery, we heard of another grave site found just on the boundary between El Carmen and the neighboring Ejido Jaboncillos. We made a quick trip early one morning over to the ejido, and walked up to the site. Only bone fragments remained. According to local residents, after a rainstorm had washed away much of the silty loam of the banks, a youngster was walking along the creek bed. The boy noticed a *metate* protruding from the creek bank at an odd angle. After digging in the soft dirt around the metate, he discovered a disintegrating skull. Curiously, the metate had been placed directly on the skull. Apparently once the skull was exposed to the air and sunlight, it began to slowly fall apart. We collected a couple of teeth and a few bone fragments.

One day in June 2003 we were working along the creek in Cañón Juárez and discovered four more graves that were slight mounds covered with stones. There were no markers of any sort, not even wooden crosses.

The archaeology of the Carmens is not well known. Many small camps and fire rings are in the lower country, whereas such evidence of human habitation in the higher country appears to be relatively sparse. In the future a detailed study will be conducted to further the knowledge on the history of this area. In the meantime, the silence of the graves, and the bones of the skeletons will remain protected in their lonely sites.

Skeleton in the desert. Photo J.D. Villalobos, 2006

25 Chihuahuan Desert Bears

All of my family, friends, and colleagues know that black bears are my favorite wildlife species. Not only are they my favorite, but I have been privileged to work with black bears first in West Texas at the Black Gap Wildlife Management Area, and now in Coahuila, Mexico, in the Carmens.

The black bear has struggled to survive in both Mexico and Texas. There are now small satellite populations beginning the recolonization process in western Texas, but it wasn't always this way. Historically the American black bear occupied most of the ecological regions of Texas, the exception being the extreme southern portion of the state, although there have been sightings as far south as the Rio Grande Valley. As European colonization and settlement expanded, the black bear began to decline. Unregulated hunting, loss of habitat, and predator control all contributed to the extirpation of this species in Texas. As long ago as 1905, Vernon Bailey conducted his biological surveys and reported that black bear were restricted to the rugged mountains and canyons of western Texas, and along the river bottoms and pine woodlands of East Texas. A few bears were still being reported on the Edwards Plateau. In the 1940s, the last stronghold of the black bear in Texas was found in the rugged Trans-Pecos, mainly in the Davis, Chisos, Chinati, Caballo del Muerto, Sierra del Carmen, and Guadalupe Mountains.

Before the 1940s, traditional fall bear hunting in West Texas yielded a good harvest. One old-timer in the Marathon area told me that in the 1930s, seven bears were killed during a single hunt in southeast Brewster County. An early attempt was made to protect the black bear in Texas in 1925 when the state legislature established a restricted hunting season, November 16 through December 31, with a bag limit of one bear per hunter per season. Bear hunting was then prohibited in all Texas counties in 1973 under the regulatory authority of the Texas Parks and Wildlife Department. In 1977, the department initiated a black bear project to evaluate habitat and to determine the actual status and distribution of black bears in Texas. In 1983, bear hunting was prohibited statewide. However, by this time, there were none left to hunt. An occasional bear would wander into West Texas, particularly in the Big Bend and Black Gap Wildlife Management Area, but they were not resident at this time.

To the south in Mexico the black bear had not fared much better. In the 1950s only a remnant population was thought to remain in the remote mountains of northern Coahuila, particularly in the Sierra del Carmen/Maderas del Carmen, Serranías del Burro, Sierra Encantada, and Sierra Santa Fé del Pino (R. Baker, pers. comm., 2007). It was during this time period that Mexican President Miguel Alemán (in office from 1946–1952) made his annual pilgrimage to the mountains of northern Coahuila for his traditional bear hunt.

He didn't see a bear, much less kill one. When he returned to Mexico City, he placed a moratorium on bear hunting throughout the country. This was the first protection that black bears in Mexico received. Many years later in 1986, the black bear was listed in Mexico as *en peligro de extinción* (endangered). Texas followed suit in 1987. Currently the black bear is listed as endangered in Mexico, with the exception of a small area in the Serranías del Burro where it is under "special protection," and Texas lists the black bear as a "state threatened species."

This brings us to the Carmen Mountain black bears, a subject near and dear to my heart. A researcher very seldom has the opportunity to study a species unhindered by politics, and the Carmen Mountain black bear study was no exception.

One of the first things we identified in Coahuila was the need for information on life history parameters, including reproduction, density, survival, home range, diet, habitat use, dispersal patterns and avenues, seasonal movement in relation to food availability, and emigration into adjacent areas and egress from Texas and the surrounding Mexican mountains. Black bear predation on domestic livestock has become a major issue for a number of ranchers and *ejidatarios* (communal property owners) in several adjacent areas, and pressure to hunt the black bear to alleviate the problem is currently an issue. However, not all black bears kill livestock, and hunting bears in a slowly recovering and expanding population is not the solution. Several bears may be killed while the "guilty" bear remains at large. It is virtually impossible to determine which bear killed livestock unless the bear is actually seen making the kill or the bear has an identifiable marker of some type.

We reviewed historical information, and current literature, interviewed ranchers, and collected information from local ejidatarios on black bears in northern Coahuila. We submitted our proposal and waited on permits. Everything finally fell into place in early 2003. In this Mexican mountain ecosystem today, bears live at all elevations, in all habitats, and can endear themselves to you or make you want to pull your hair out with their latest escapades.

A typical scenario for a bear-trapping day in the Carmens goes something like this. We load the equipment, extra bait, socks (for bait bags), lunch, water, data sheets, and telemetry equipment, and then gas up the truck and head to the sierra. It is September 2005, the desert country is hot, and the bears are using canyons and the higher elevations. Fruits are ripening, acorns are ready, and along with all the adult bears there are the yearlings the sows weaned off in June and July. I have the nondirectional antenna on top of the truck to pick up remote locations, and shortly I hear the first beep: Chica, a young sow with a cub, is going about her daily routine feeding in the mid-elevations.

The radio crackles and Hugo says that a bear—a small yearling, maybe a female—has been caught at the road to the Mesa de los Fresnos. We turn around and head back down the mountain. When daytime temperatures are hot, we need to work up any captured bears in the lower elevations first. We head into Cañón el Álamo and drive up the canyon. The road is covered in bear tracks of all sizes, a regular bear highway. We arrive at the trap site; the barrel trap is in the shade and the bear is comfortable, but very ticked off. The little female is huffing and popping her teeth and bouncing all over the inside of the barrel, which is making it very difficult for us to give her the immobilizing injection with the jab stick. Finally, she decides to move to the middle of the trap where she rolls over on her back, sticks all four feet in the air, and does her daily aerobics while we stand by waiting on her to move to one or the other end of the trap. When at last she makes her move, shortly she is asleep and we are working her up. She is in good condition, and as we affix her radio collar and take the last data, she begins to move around as she slowly wakes up. We mist her with cool water, keeping her body temperature down in the stifling heat of mid-morning. She moves off, disappearing into the brush. She has a number and a frequency so we can monitor her, but her name is Serena.

We clean the equipment, load everything back in the truck, and head down the canyon, cutting across at the *Pila* Jaime and starting the climb up-

Marina, radio-collared female with cub. Photo J. D. Villalobos, 2007

ward. We round the turn at Los Cojos and see Chica and her cub of the year on the slope; she is also in good condition. Farther up we check the barrel traps we have out on the mountain, and find nothing until we get to Cuadra Pelota. There is no doubt that a bear is inside and apparently a big one. Sure enough, we have caught a very large and quite tranquil male. We inject him and tug him out of the trap inch by inch. He is inky black, so black his coat looks blue in the rays of sunlight filtering through the pines and firs. His chest bears a large white mark, one of the few with such marks. His head is huge; he doesn't appear to be very old, as his teeth are relatively white and show little wear. We name him Santana. The work-up is easy and then we pull him into

deeper shade. He is slowly waking up and content to just lie in the shade and watch us.

Santana is a new bear to this area; we haven't seen him before, nor his tracks, which are huge. We wait in the shade having a late lunch. The breeze is from the south and warm, the scent of warm pine resin fills the air. I breathe deeply, I love the smell of pines in the woods, winter or summer. We don't have a long wait, as he decides to get up and moves off quickly—it's amazing how a three-hundred-pound black bear can vanish without a trace in seconds. I wonder about his home range. Judging by the direction he is heading, maybe he spends his time in the high country and over toward the east side of Centinela. Only telemetry and time will tell.

We call Campo Uno on the radio and David reports that we haven't caught any bears in the traps there but that he saw two bears this morning, one with a collar and one without. We tell David that we are headed to Uno to rebait the traps and check telemetry. The radio signal from the Campo Uno area indicates another male, Tecate. We have a quick cup of coffee with David; it is mid-afternoon. We check telemetry here and up at La Laguna and then begin the long drive back to Pilares. We stop and check telemetry, pick up scats, mark their location, and see more bears without collars. A yearling crosses the road running full tilt, disappearing into the forest in seconds. Below La Cachuchua we see another

Captured and radio-collared black bear. Photo J. D. Villalobos, 2005

yearling. Trapping will be good this month with all the yearlings running around. They are all hungry and having to fend for themselves for the first time in their lives. It was a good day, as we had captured and radio-collared two more bears for the study, a yearling and a large male.

We reached Pilares headquarters around 7:00 p.m. after stopping many times to check telemetry. The bears were moving everywhere; it was dry and food sources were scarcer this year. I checked my email and called Bill on the radio to tell him I was headed to San Isidro. He replied, and said he'd seen a big bear below the Pila Chebo with no collar. I headed home looking for the bear but didn't see him.

Bear trapping can be very good one day and lousy the next, or bears may walk right by the traps for several days or even weeks. However, this wasn't the case in the fall of 2005. With the dry conditions, bears were moving all over the mountain and the lower country searching for food. We were capturing bears practically every day—one, two, three, and our best day, four.

The day, September 24, 2005, started out in typical fashion: gas the truck, gather up equipment, clean the equipment box, and refurbish supplies. Yesterday we had captured three bears; we got in around 9:00 p.m., tired but happy bear trappers. Once we had all the stuff loaded, we started for the mountain to check all the traps and telemetry. Bill and Salvador were ahead of us and radioed back that we had a big bear in the trap at Casa Negro. We arrived and Beto joined us, as he

was close by in the canyon. The trap's interior was dark, as it was in the shade, and the big male was very tranquil, napping in the coolness. We could see he had a radio collar and it was pretty snug. We decided to check the collar, and while he was going under the anesthesia, I checked radio signals trying to identify the bear. We had caught Villa a year and a half ago when he was a yearling. He had moved up into the west Jardín area, and during the past winter we had lost radio-signal contact on him. I had wondered whether he went farther and crossed into Texas or moved into the adjacent mountains in Coahuila. The spacer on his collar was just about ready to break, being held together by a couple of threads. Because the collar had become snug and rubbed several places bare on his neck, we opted not to recollar him. We had a lot of data from his locations. We worked him up and waited while he recovered completely and walked off.

We headed on toward the top of the mountain, but then Beto called on the radio. A bear had been caught at Chamiceras. Back down the mountain we went; we could check the rest of the mountain traps later, as they were in the shade and in the higher elevations the temperatures were cooler. Even though the barrel was in the shade in Chamiceras, we didn't want the bear to overheat. We made it down the mountain in record time and headed to Chamiceras. We parked the truck and packed our equipment in a short distance. We had caught a young male; he was a little thin but in good condition. We named him

Flaco and worked him up. Beto remained with him until he recovered.

It was now 2:30 p.m., and we still had all the traps to check from Casa Negro to Campo Uno. The Campo Cinco barrel was closed; we had another bear there and for want of a better name, he was dubbed Cinco. We worked him up quickly, waited on him to recover, and headed toward Uno. The next barrel, another bear, and that made four in one day! This was another young male; we named him Bravo because of his attitude. You would have thought there was a huge bear inside this trap upon hearing his huffing and teeth popping.

It was getting late and we still had five traps to check. We put Bravo back in the barrel to recover and closed the door. On the way back we would open the door and he could leave the area fully recovered. We bounced and jounced over the rough road to Uno and La Laguna; no bears but many tracks in the road. On the way back up the mountain toward Divisadero we saw another bear without a collar. It was dusk and I was checking telemetry. Frida was in her usual spot; Lupita was in Carboneras, toward the Puerta Linces; Chaco's and Domingo's signals were faint, as they were in the canyon below. We reached Divisadero and released Bravo; he huffed off into the approaching darkness in no better mood than earlier in the day. His feelings were sure ruffled for a little guy.

I slumped down in the seat and poured the last cup of half-warm coffee. We headed down

Male black bear, Sierra del Carmen.
Photo B. P. McKinney, 2010

the mountain still checking telemetry, and picked up Porfirio, Santana, Vico, Chica, Cinco, Pacifico, Macarena, and Caliente. A good bear day but a very long one. Coming off the mountain in the darkness with the bear frequencies beeping softly in my headset, I was lost in thought. This population of bears was definitely increasing. When we moved here in 2001, we saw bears, one here and one there; in the fall a couple in this canyon and a few in that canyon; we saw a few cubs and yearlings. Now we are seeing bears and more bears.

For the first time in probably one hundred

years, a very large portion of the Carmen Mountains now offers a haven not only to bears but all species. Hunting pressure is gone, habitats are recovering from many years of overabuse, and the bears are thriving in this situation. Will we be overpopulated? No, I don't think so, as they have room to expand, and through normal dispersal bears will continue to move in all directions. I am waiting for the day when one of our collared study bears moves across the Rio Grande. Ground telemetry in the high country of the Carmens is difficult, given the deep canyons, ravines, mountains, cliffs, and rock piles. Oftentimes when a bear disperses a long distance, we will lose their signal and it may be months before we locate the animal with ground telemetry. However, through the generosity of CEMEX, El Carmen now has a single-engine plane based at the project site. We will use it for radio telemetry work, not only on bears but bighorns and elk as well, and for checking project lands.

Since I began work here at El Carmen, not only has the bear population grown, but the project has more than tripled in size and is still growing. Much of the corridor country that previously presented many perils to dispersing black bears is now under direct ownership of CEMEX and El Carmen. The corridors now offer safe travel on both sides of the Carmens for almost the complete distance from the Cuesta Malena to the Rio Grande. Ranchers and ejidos all know about the bear project, and all have been extremely hospi-

table in allowing us to access their properties to pick up radio collars that fell off of bears when the spacers broke. They have allowed us to conduct telemetry and use their roads, and have told us some great stories while sharing their coffee. We appreciate all their hospitality and their willingness to work with us, and not against us, in bear conservation.

There will always be people on both sides of the border who will kill black bears, whether from fear based on stories about killing livestock, or in illegal hunts. A number of bears will continue to die needlessly every year. Fortunately, there are lands in both countries that afford the black bear protection. There are biologists and managers in both countries willing to work with landowners so that they can coexist with black bears. Bears can and do cause problems. However, many of the problems are created by humans or can be prevented by humans. Bears are super-intelligent animals, and when they see an opportunity for an easy meal, they will take it.

Livestock depredation does occur, especially in years when natural foods are in low supply and on lands that are overgrazed or in rotation grazing systems. I have noticed that in the case of rotation systems where depredation is occurring, often the water supply is cut off in the area from which the cattle are being moved. In effect, the bears move with the cattle since they too need water. The problem escalates when calving coincides with bears coming out of winter hibernation in early spring. Cows will leave calves unattended under a sotol or other vegetation and graze away from the calf. Bears then walk by and lunch on a newborn calf. One rancher who changed his calving time to later in the spring reduced depredation from bears by 70 percent in a single calving season. Consequently, he continues to ensure that his cows calve in late spring.

Some of the depredation is created by human practices. For instance, landowners who put out feed for deer and other wildlife literally habituate bears to their cattle operations and their houses and outbuildings. Bears love deer feeders and are close to geniuses in deriving ways to empty them. The landowner gets mad at the bear, the bear gets mad because his free meals are gone, the landowner goes for his rifle, the bear goes for the dog food or the horse feed in the barn and all hell breaks loose. Rule number one is, do not feed the bears: a fed bear is a dead bear. Common sense in dealing with bears goes a long way. Bears and humans coexist in many states in the United States with few problems. I grew up in bear country in Virginia and cannot recall problem bears; they were well-mannered forest bears, not junkies looking for a free meal at a deer feeder. Bears are an integral part of the Mexican and West Texas landscape. They belong here, and if landowners give them a chance and learn how to prevent conflicts before they happen, bears can once again roam historic range in both countries.

I feel very privileged to have been able to conduct research on a species that was absent from historic range in western Texas for close to fifty years and then returned on their own and began to reestablish a small population. I feel even more privileged to live in the Sierra del Carmen of Coahuila, and be able to watch a bear with her three cubs moving up the slope across the arroyo from my house in April, or to observe a fat bear sitting in a pool of cool mountain water with an expression on his face akin to pure pleasure as the water cools him off. I feel blessed when upon turning a corner in the road going down the canyon from Casa San Isidro, I see a very large old sow with four cubs following her down the road. She crosses the road, grunting to the cubs to hurry along; they scamper after her, short tails tucked. They are part of the future bear populations for this mountain and adjacent mountains in Mexico and western Texas. I am only a small player in the grand plan; the bears are the major players and it is up to many people in both countries to see that there are places left for a sow to den in December, birth her cubs, and bring them forth into the outdoors in late April.

When habitats support a large population of black bears, it is an indicator of habitat well-being as it is supporting the largest animal in the ecosystem. Bears won't stay in country that doesn't support them with food sources, water, cover, den sites, and room to roam. Here in the Carmens they have all that and protection as well.

For almost five years we had been working steadily on all phases of the flora and fauna baseline inventory for the Carmens when we realized in 2005 that we were lacking information on butterflies, which were everywhere in the spring through the fall months. We began fieldwork documenting the presence of species and collecting specimens. We had much other fieldwork to conduct on various research projects and baseline inventory, so we would pack up the butterfly collecting gear along with our other field equipment. When we saw butterflies, we would stop and take photos and collect.

There are many different habitats for butterflies in the Carmens, as well as abundant water and food sources. Many migrants move through these mountains, as well as strays from farther south. Our list was growing daily, and we were pretty confident of our identification for most. We were delighted when Ro and Betty Wauer, Jim Brock, and Sally and Eric Fickelstein came for a visit. We had much to learn about butterflies and Jim and Ro were the experts. We spent as much time as possible with them, and they helped us identify several species we were not sure of.

Butterfly collecting is a science; butterflies seem to float effortlessly along, so we thought they would be easy to catch. We learned quickly that you just didn't step out of the truck and gently scoop up a butterfly. Amid much jumping, running, falling down, and unusual dance antics we were slowly improving our technique on butterfly capture. How could you miss a huge swallowtail butterfly with a big net when it was at eye level floating along? Very easily—I must have missed dozens. Each new species we added to the list was a small victory and our list continued to grow.

Early in June 2005, we were on a ridge above Los Cojos and saw a medium-size butterfly rise up from Pringle's speargrass and fly to another patch of grass. Jonás and I asserted simultaneously that *this* was a different butterfly. So we left the truck and commenced our weird dance of catch-the-butterfly. "Dancing with the Stars" contestants had nothing on us. We could turn, hop, swoop, twirl, glide, moonwalk, jitterbug, and tango after a butterfly, and we were getting better at it. Almost simultaneously we netted two specimens. Jonás dropped his net about ten seconds before I dropped mine. We prepared the specimens; we were not sure of the identification as it was similar to Ridings' satyr but somewhat different in both wing color and pattern shape on the wing. The habitat preference of the newly captured butterfly was the windswept ridges above La Cachuchua and below Casa Negro in pine-oak woodland habitat. We took photos of habitat, the Pringle speargrass, and of the butterfly itself.

Ro and Betty Wauer, Jim Brock, and Eric and Sally Fickelstein made their annual visit to El Carmen in August. After studying the two specimens we had collected, Jim was sure this species was

JoBoni satyr. Photo Jim Brock, 2007

different. Working under permits issued by the Universidad Nacional Autónoma de México (UNAM), we collected more specimens and carefully prepared them to send to Mexico City. I asked Salvador to hand carry the package to Monterrey and then have them ship it overnight to Mexico City to Jorge Llorente at UNAM. Then we anxiously awaited the DNA results. Andy Warren emailed me in late 2007 to inform me that it was definitely a new species. This new species differed from Ridings satyr by wing color, shape, and pattern of markings on the wing, and in the genitalia of both males and females. DNA analysis confirmed the differences compared to other *Neominois* species. In the meantime we had been referring to this species as the JoBoni satyr. We mulled over many common names before we settled on JoBoni. Jonás dropped his net seconds before I did, so he got the honor of being first in the common name, so "JoBoni satyr" it became. The most exciting part of discovering a new species to science was the fact that the common name is not only named after us, but the scientific name is *Neominois carmen*, named after the Carmen Mountains, a new tribute to the mountain. I am sure there are more species to be discovered, especially butterflies and plants. It would take another entire lifetime to document the insect life.

Currently we have baseline information on over 140 species of butterflies for the Carmen Mountains, including a couple that may be new subspecies. In 2008, the scientific paper was published in *Zootaxa* announcing the new species found in northeastern Mexico, the JoBoni satyr.

27 Billy Pat and the Flying Bug

Billy Pat, my husband of over thirty years, did not enter middle age by suddenly feeling the need to buy a sports car, head to the bar, and chase women. Instead, he woke up one morning with the flying bug. He was raised among people who flew airplanes more than they drove cars—both his dad and his uncle Clayton were excellent pilots, but he hadn't been interested then. The bug bit him when we had a visit from Vico Gutiérrez.

Vico is a great ultralight pilot, having flown in many different places around the world, and in the fall of 2005 he began a journey that was nothing other than stunning. Following the migration of the monarch butterfly, he flew from Canada to the state of Michoacán, Mexico in an ultralight. During his trip he called and asked if he could stop for several days at El Carmen. We said, of course, but we were not on the regular monarch migration path. He said he really wanted to come back and visit the Carmens, as he had been there years before and had not forgotten the beauty of the mountains.

Vico arrived with his ultralight, accompanied by another ultralight and a crew of six people. We were delighted to have them, and he was ready to fly any of us who wanted to go. Naturally, many of us wanted to fly the Carmens in his ultralight. The ultralight, painted exactly like a monarch, was a delightful spectacle—imagine a huge monarch butterfly wafting along on the wind. My flight was nothing short of breathtaking. Sitting behind Vico we took off from the Pilares airstrip and started gaining altitude rapidly to the tune of eight hundred feet a minute. The motor hummed along, we were flying high—I loved it. After climbing over the top of the Carmens at an altitude of about ten thousand feet, we then swooped down into the spires of rhyolite on the east side of Centinela Peak, turning and twisting among the spires, then out over the desert, and later back to land at Pilares. Armando Galindo, Veronica Ruiz, Jonás Delgadillo, Hugo Sotelo, Beto Martinez, Mauro Alonso, and several others flew with Vico and the other pilot. Billy Pat also flew, which was when the flying bug bit him, although at the time I was not aware of the "bite." We had a great visit with Vico and dinner at our house before they flew out on October 8, 2005.

Shortly thereafter, a glaze appeared in my husband's eyes and he kept the computer hot Googling for information on and visuals of ultralights. True, we needed a plane at El Carmen since we were far from a hospital, and we could also survey wildlife, check boundaries, and do aerial telemetry. Suddenly the coffee table at our house was piled high with aviation information. One day, he dropped in at my office and said, "I am going to learn to fly." I replied, "Okay!"

First were the online courses for ground school. I learned more about Cessna airplanes than I ever wanted to know, as well as air speeds, weather, clouds, wind, and controls. Every night we went over information after dinner. There was no watching television, no reading, and no painting—all we did was review ground school information and practice test questions. The questions became our nightly entertainment. Finally, he was off to Castorville to take the ground school test; he passed with flying colors, making the highest grade in the class. The hunt for an airplane was on. CEMEX had agreed to purchase a small plane. I studied photos of airplanes from Canada to Mexico, as I was getting good at flyers' language about icing, wind speed, runway numbers, and tail numbers. The search for a flying instructor began and one was located in Del Rio, our port of entry into the United States. So off he went to flying school. I will always remember the first flight he made on the first day of flying school. Our house in Del Rio is just a pasture and fence away from the runway at Del Rio International, so there I was with binoculars watching him during his first lesson. I admit some surprise; I saw him get into the pilot's seat and then shortly they took off. He looked like a pro. Lessons continued while I was in the Carmens and he went to Del Rio. Finally, the day of the flying test came and he passed that also.

In the meantime, CEMEX had purchased a Cessna 182 Wren with a STOL kit and outfitted with excellent geographic positioning systems (GPS). It was painted like a Holstein cow, black and white spots; all it needed was a pink udder. Shortly that was changed to a beautiful two-tone green and white. Having obtained his U.S. pilot's license, he was now off to Monterrey, Mexico to get his Mexican pilot's license since the plane was registered in Mexico. Flying lessons went well and soon he had his Mexican pilot's license.

It was the week before Christmas 2006; I had left El Carmen on the twenty-first in the morning to drive to Del Rio for the holiday. Billy Pat was still in Monterrey, but called and said he would be flying in to Del Rio the next afternoon with his instructor from Monterrey. I couldn't wait—finally he would make that first international flight! I was pacing the driveway by 2:00 p.m. Finally at about 3:30 p.m., I saw the plane coming in and headed to the airport. He touched down and landed then headed to the circle to clear U.S. Customs. He was glad all the instruction was completed and ready to fly the Wren to learn that particular airplane.

New pilots have a lot to learn. Every model seems to have its very own quirks, and the Wren was no different. Coy Ziehe, our friend and long-time pilot came to visit, and he and Bill decided they would fly the Wren the next day. They headed out in early afternoon, the wind came up, and I was wondering how they were doing. Later that afternoon they flew back to Del Rio, and Pam Bunch joined us and we visited at our house, where the talk was all about airplanes. They had a good flight and some high-wind conditions.

The next week Billy Pat's dad joined us in Del Rio, and they flew together which was neat since

Billy Pat Sr. had flown about a jillion hours. They laughed and joked and headed to El Carmen for a few days of practice flying there. The first flight I made with Billy Pat, we had turbulence and a bumpy landing at Pilares, but an okay flight. Now he is a seasoned and a careful pilot; he and "Ol' Wrenny" take off and land like a feather. The plane enables us to fly telemetry, fires, boundary checks, and wildlife surveys, and of course, we can fly a person out of El Carmen to a hospital if necessary.

Never in my wildest dreams would I have imagined Bill becoming a pilot, and one that loves

Billy Pat and the Cessna 182 Wren, 2006

flying so much that I can honestly say he is addicted to it. The Carmens and adjacent Serranías del Burro are not easy mountains to fly in a small plane. The updrafts, downdrafts, and general turbulence test a pilot's skills. Billy Pat learned his flying skills over these mountains. Just ask him about the time when just as he touched down on the runway and a whirlwind got under the tail of the plane. He tells that story much better than I.

28 The Pronghorn Returns

The pronghorn was extirpated from a large portion of its historic range in Mexico many years ago. Problems associated with the extirpation process included loss of large tracts of grassland habitat, fences, and overhunting. Pronghorns need large amounts of space to run, and loss of native grasslands and the barbed-wired fences that restricted their movement were probably the major factors in their decline. Predation of fawns by coyotes and other carnivores contributed to the extirpation; normally a pronghorn can outrun most predators but when faced with fences their odds for survival decline drastically.

Efforts to reintroduce the pronghorn to northern Coahuila began in Valle Colombia in 1996, which is just across the valley from the Carmens. In our long-range management plan we had included the pronghorn for reintroduction, but needed to restore the lower grasslands to support this species. Work began in 2004 with the use of the Lawson aerator, which punches holes in the soil, breaking the hard, eroded top layer while also crunching unwanted vegetation, and allows the soil to breathe and hold rainwater for seed ger-

Pronghorns at El Carmen, 2009

mination. Even after several years of resting, many thousands of acres at El Carmen remained eroded, hard-packed soil dotted with creosote bush, tarbush, and prickly pear cactus. The aerator went to work; some areas were reseeded with native grasses while others were left to see if a seed bank remained under the hard-packed soil. After abundant rains, the grassland was returning faster than we imagined possible—not only grass, but also weeds, forbs, and wildflowers. The diversity in species was what pronghorn needed, along with other wildlife and seed-eating birds. Grasses make up only a small portion of the pronghorn diet; they prefer a diverse diet of annual forbs and weeds as well. The lands we were working on were coming back as we hoped. We also developed water sources.

In 2009 the opportunity arose for El Carmen to make a trade with the New Mexico Game and Fish Department (NMGF) as a part of three groups in Coahuila that would receive pronghorn. This effort was supported by the Secretaría del Medio Ambiente, Recursos Naturales y Pesca, Comisión Nacional de Áreas Naturales Protegidas, and a host of other agencies. The El Carmen crew headed to New Mexico in early March 2009; the first year's capture resulted in forty-five animals for El Carmen and like numbers for the other two groups. The fawn crop in 2009 was a good one and we had hopes of returning to New Mexico for another fifty-five pronghorn in 2010. Again, in March 2010 we headed to New Mexico

and the capture went well. NMGF did a great job at the capture site, and we headed back through Texas on our way home to the Carmens. By the end of fawning season in June, we expected to have a stable population from which to expand. The pronghorn is a captivating species, as they seem to run effortlessly across the grasslands and often gaze into the distance at rain storms and far mountains. They are an integral part of the fauna of northern Mexico and are once again grazing on spring wildflowers and weeds in historic habitat.

Restored grasslands, 2009

29 Doc Baker's Visit— July 2007

The late Rollin Baker was my mentor, friend, and endless source of information on mammals of Coahuila. Doc Baker and I began corresponding in the early 1990s when Chabela Sellers and I launched a bird project on her ranch in the Serranías del Burro, directly across the valley from the Carmen Mountains in Coahuila. He generously sent me one of his last copies of *The Mammals of Coahuila*, and also many of his reprints of published articles on mammals in Mexico over the years. After moving to Coahuila in 2001, nearly every Monday morning I would have an email from Doc detailing an area to look for a certain mammal or other mountains to explore, and checking on my progress with baseline inventory in the Carmens.

Doc knew much about the old ranches in northern Coahuila, including the Las Margaritas Ranch, formerly owned by the family of Chabela Sellers and her brother Roberto. He traveled in the Carmen Mountains via the old road out of Acuña, Coahuila, which led to the east side of the Carmens, where he and his crew documented the first specimen of the Coahuila mole at El Club.

I had pestered him for years to come and visit us in the Carmens, but he wasn't in the best of health and did not know if he could make the trip. Several years later in April 2007, he emailed me that he had tons of journals that he would like to gift us with if we would pick them up. Of course I replied that we would do so. Billy Pat and I rented a small U-Haul trailer and shortly headed to Eagle Lake. I finally got to meet Doc Baker in person, and he, Billy Pat, and I had a great visit while we loaded up boxes and boxes of journals. I was thrilled to have them, as they are valuable reference materials that are now immediately accessible at El Carmen. Before we left, he promised to visit us.

On July 15, 2007, I met him and daughter Betsy in Del Rio. We headed south on the highway, and then on an *autopista* (expressway); Doc could not believe we weren't jouncing over a dirt road. I had a surprise waiting for him in Múzquiz. I had contacted Chabela, and she and her brother and husband Charlie would meet us for a late lunch at El Jacal. We reached Múzquiz and I pulled into a parking space at El Jacal, telling my passengers that we would have lunch here before continuing on to El Carmen. Doc truly was delightedly surprised, and reminisced about the old days in Coahuila with Chabela and Roberto, who had been children when he met them in 1950s. Once we finished lunch, we headed northwest to the Carmens. All along the way he talked about fieldwork in many areas and pointed out old ranches; he was a walking encyclopedia on wildlife in this area over a half-century in the past.

We reached the Carmen gate and had a photo session, and then on to Pilares headquarters where the first thing he wanted to see was the Coahuila mole. I introduced him to the biologist and we headed up the canyon to our house. He

Doc Baker at El Carmen.
Photo B. P. McKinney, July 2007

was in seventh heaven and very happy to be back in the Carmens. We had coffee on the patio and he was continually taking field notes. In fact, Doc was ready to head out into the field the next morning. We drove to Pilares to pick up Jonás and then headed up to the high country. Doc marveled at the changes—the grasses were coming back and the wildlife was visible. He remarked that the mule deer we were observing were the first live mule deer he had seen in Coahuila. We stopped at Cuadra Pelota and showed him where we found the Miller's shrew nest. In short order he was looking for pocket gopher tunnels, and then on his hands and knees exploring their runways.

We then headed to Campo Uno and again he was pleasantly surprised by the changes in this part of the mountain. Returning to Casa San Isidro in late afternoon, we took a coffee break on the patio. The biologist came up for dinner, and afterward Doc took the floor. He had converted

Roberto Spence, Doc Baker, Chabela Spence Sellers, and Bonnie McKinney (standing), Múzquiz, Coahuila. Photo B. P. McKinney, July 2007

several of his old eight-track videos to DVDs and we had a great evening while he showed us his Mexican field trips during the 1950s.

The next day we headed out early to the east side of the Carmens back to Doc's old stomping grounds at El Club and Hacienda Piedra Blanca. We had been bear trapping in the El Club area, and we had called Fernando at El Club on the radio and told him to please open and bait the barrel traps in hopes of catching a bear while Doc was there. Early in the day Fernando called on the radio reporting that we had a bear. We hurried to the other side of the mountain and into the canyon complex where El Club is located. Shortly, we were immobilizing the bear and working him up. Doc told us that this was the first live black bear he had seen in Coahuila; in the 1950s they were scarce, he said, he had seen only dead bears and a few old skulls. We worked the bear up and he took photos while Betsy made a video.

Fernando and his wife Ellie made a great lunch. Later Doc talked about his field trips into this area, and then we hiked up the canyon a ways to where he found the Coahuila mole in nearly the same place we did. We loaded up in the truck and headed down canyon and took the road to Hacienda Piedra Blanca. When Doc was there, it was an active ranch and the hacienda was in livable condition. We hiked around, took many photos, and headed out for the west side amid a thunderstorm and rain.

The next several days we showed as much of the Carmens as we could to Doc Baker. We had great visits, and talked late into the night each and every day. The final morning we had a late breakfast, packed, and headed back to Del Rio. I only hope he enjoyed that visit as much as we did, and I hope he knew how much I learned from him over the years.

For some time Doc and I had been bantering back and forth about a book he had. I had wanted to read Young and Goldman's *Wolves of North America* for many years, and Doc had a copy. He kept telling me that he would let me read it "one of these days." In October 2007, after his visit in July I received a package in the mail at Del Rio from Doc. Inside was a note: "The book is yours, I want you to have it." I emailed him my many thanks. That was the last correspondence I had with Doc. Shortly thereafter he was hospitalized; the cancer had returned and his health was failing. We called his daughter and emailed her, keeping up with his condition. Sadly, I received an email early in November, on the day before his birthday, saying that he passed away.

I miss Doc Baker's Monday morning emails and the banter we engaged in. He was a generous, kind man, and a great mammalogist. A couple of days before Christmas 2007, I was in Del Rio and had stopped by the post office to pick up the mail. As I sorted through it, I noticed an envelope with his address stamped on it. Thinking it was from Betsy his daughter, I opened it, and there it was, a picture of him at El Carmen and his annual Christmas card. Never one to lose his sense of humor, among other things the card read, "This year has been tough on me." *Descanso*, Doc, you worked hard and enlightened many of us.

30 A Final Note

As I write this final note, I hope I have been able to give you a glimpse of the Carmens—magical, mystical, mythical, mysterious, never-ending beauty in a vast mountain range, so close and yet at times so far that you can only dream about it. The name alone evokes images burned into my memory for all time. There is no place like the Carmens and there will never be another; this one is so precious that it must be protected at all costs. It is an ecosystem that deserves recognition for being one of the most uniquely diverse areas of the great Chihuahuan Desert. It would not be recovering in as many areas as it is today were it not for CEMEX, a private corporation willing to take on the costly and long-term commitment to restore this grand old mountain range. I wish to personally thank CEMEX for all the resources, time, and effort thus far, and for the promise to make the Carmens a legacy for generations to come in preserving the biodiversity of this great place.

The contiguous lands in Coahuila; the Sierra Santa Rosa, Sierra Encantada, Serranías del Burro, Loma de Colorado, Sierra San Vicente, and the Carmens; in Chihuahua, the Sierra Santa Fé del Pino, Sierra de Hechiceros, and Sierra

Making tracks. Photo J. D. Villalobos, 2005

Rica; sky islands surrounded by Chihuahuan Desert; and in West Texas; the Caballo del Muerto, and the Sierras del Carmen, Chisos, Christmas, Glass, Del Nortes, Housetops, Solitario, Chinati—all are part of a great transboundary conservation effort. It may be one of the most significant in the world. The ecological corridors that these mountain ranges in both countries support are of utmost importance for the continued existence of wildlife species moving during dispersal and normal range expansion. Without contiguous lands on both sides of the border, conservation is hampered. If conservation stops at the Rio Bravo del Norte, then many efforts will be futile. It takes international cooperation by federal and state agencies and the landowners in both countries to fight the battle for preserving lands for flora and fauna (Culver et al., 2009). Unless all entities work together, we fight a losing battle. CEMEX has taken the lead in this large conservation project in Mexico. They have set the example and hopefully other corporations and nongovernmental agencies will follow their lead. The same is true in West Texas; habitat and wildlife conservation is something that all of us should be willing to support. Would we want to show our grandchildren and great grandchildren a picture of a red-tailed hawk in a book only, because there were none left in the wild? Perhaps you think this is extreme, but time marches on very fast, we are losing species at an alarming rate all over the world, and it is mostly due to habitat loss. Trans-

boundary conservation by two great countries like Mexico and the United States can be a model to be duplicated all over the world. What we are working for today in wildlife conservation is the legacy we will leave subsequent generations.

I am alone tonight; the canyon is quiet and it is cold. I walk outside with my last cup of coffee, and the moon is full over the mountaintop, the stars twinkle in the dark sky, no lights mar the view, an owl calls softly and another answers. This is the way it should be, and the way I hope it will be for many more years. No, the lobo has not yet returned, but there is still time. I hope with all my heart that one night in the future I can walk outside with my last cup of coffee, the moon will be full, it will be cold, and I will hear the drawn-out, lonesome howl of a lobo echo down the canyon. Then the mountain will finally rest—all will once again be in its place, all in balance.

Common and Scientific Names Used in the Text

Mammals

Common Name	Scientific Name
American black bear	*Ursus americanus*
Big brown bat	*Eptesicus fuscus*
Black-tailed jackrabbit	*Lepus californicus*
Bobcat	*Lynx rufus*
Botta's pocket gopher	*Thomomys bottae*
Brazilian free-tailed bat	*Nyctinomops femorosaccus*
Carmen Mountain white-tailed deer	*Odocoileus virginianus carminis*
Cliff chipmunk	*Eutamia dorsalis*
Coahuila mole	*Scalopus aquaticus montanus*
Collared peccary	*Pecari tajacu*
Common gray fox	*Urocyon cinereoargenteus*
Coyote	*Canis latrans*
Deer mouse	*Peromyscus maniculatus*
Desert bighorn	*Ovis canadensis mexicana*
Desert cottontail	*Sylvilagus audubonii*
Eastern fox squirrel	*Sciurus niger*
Eastern pipistrelle	*Pipistrellus subflavus*
Eastern red bat	*Lasiurus borealis*
Elk	*Cervus elaphus*
Ghost-faced bat	*Mormoops megalophylla*
Grizzly bear	*Ursus arctos*
Hoary bat	*Lasiurus cinereus*
Jaguar	*Pantera onca*

Jaguarundi	*Herpailurus yaguarondi*
Long-legged myotis	*Motis volans*
Mexican lobo	*Canis lupus baileyi*
Mexican long-eared bat	*Corynorhinus mexicanus*
Mexican long-nosed bat	*Leptonycteris nivalis*
Mexican woodrat	*Neotoma mexicana*
Miller's shrew	*Sorex milleri*
Mule deer	*Odocoileus hemionus*
North American porcupine	*Erethizon dorsatum*
Ocelot	*Leopardus pardalis*
Pallid bat	*Antrozous pallidus*
Pronghorn	*Antilocapra americana*
Puma	*Puma concolor*
Ringtail	*Bassariscus astutus*
Spotted bat	*Euderma maculatum*
Striped skunk	*Mephitis mephitis*
Townsend's big-eared bat	*Corynorhinus townsendii*
Western pipistrelle	*Pipistrellus hesperus*
Western spotted skunk	*Spilogale gracilis*
Western yellow bat	*Lasiurus ega*
White-ankled mouse	*Peromyscus pectoralis*
White-nosed coati	*Nasua narica*
Yuma myotis	*Motis yumanensis*

Plants

Common Name	Scientific Name
Alkali sacaton	*Sporobolus airoides*
Arizona cypress	*Cupressus arizonica*
Beaked yucca	*Yucca rostrata*
Beargrass	*Nolina erumpens*
Big-tooth maple	*Acer grandidentatum*
Blue grama	*Bouteloua gracilis*

Candelilla	*Euphorbia antisyphilitica*
Cardinal flower	*Lobelia cardinalis*
Chino grama	*Bouteloua breviseta*
Coahuila fir	*Abies coahuilensis*
Cottonwood	*Populus wislizenii*
Creosote bush	*Larrea tridentata*
Dakota vervain	*Verbena* sp.
Desert baileya	*Baileya multiradiata*
Dogweed	*Dyssodiopsis tagetoides*
Dogwood	*Cornus* sp.
Douglas fir	*Pseudotsuga menziesii*
Evergreen sumac	*Rhus virens*
Giant white dagger	*Yucca carnerosana*
Godding's willow	*Salix nigra*
Green sprangletop	*Leptochloa dubia*
Guayule	*Parthenium argentatum*
Havard's agave	*Agave havardiana*
Honey mesquite	*Prosopis glandulosa*
Horsetail	*Equisetum* sp.
Huisache	*Acacia smallii*
Indian paintbrush	*Castilleja nervata*
Lechuguilla	*Agave lechuguilla*
Littleleaf leadtree	*Leucaena retusa*
Long-petal echeveria	*Echeveria strictiflora*
Madroño	*Arbutus xalapensis*
Manca caballo cactus	*Coryphantha poselgeriana*
Mariola	*Parthenium incanum*
Mescal bean	*Sophora secundiflora*
Mexican basswood	*Tilia* sp.
Mexican golden oak	*Quercus sideroxla*
Mexican persimmon	*Diospyros texana*
Mexican pinyon	*Pinus cembroides*

Mexican pistachio	*Pistacia texana*
Mexican primrose	*Oenothera speciosa*
Mexican redbud	*Cercis canadensis* var. *mexicana*
Mexican squawroot	*Conopholis mexicana*
Milkweed	*Asclepias* sp.
Mountain muhly	*Muhlenbergia montana*
Mountain nine-bark	*Physocarpus monogynus*
Ocotillo	*Fouqueria splendens*
Orange mushrooom	*Boletus* sp.
Peyote	*Lopohora williamsii*
Pinyon rice grass	*Piptochaetium fimbriatum*
Pitaya cactus	*Echinocereus stramineus*
Plains bristlegrass	*Setaria macrostachya*
Plains prickly pear	*Opuntia polycantha* var. *polycantha*
Point-leaf manzanita	*Arctostaphylos pungens*
Ponderosa pine	*Pinus arizonica* var. *stormiae*
Prickly pear	*Opuntia* sp.
Pringle's speargrass	*Piptochaetium pringlei*
Quaking aspen	*Populus tremolides*
Red-flowered agave	*Agave potrerana*
Side-oats grama	*Bouteloua curtipendula* var. *caespitosa*
Slim-footed maguey	*Agave gracilipes*
Sotol	*Dasylirion leiophyllum*
Southwestern chokecherry	*Prunus serotina* var. *rufula*
Stewart's gilia	*Gilia stewartii*
Tasajillo	*Cylindopuntia leptocaulis*
Texas vervain	*Verbena officinale* ssp. *halei*
Tough-leaved sumac	*Rhus virens* ssp. *choriophylla*
Uña de gato	*Acacia greggii*
Viejito	*Echinocereus longisetus*
Virginia creeper	*Parthenocissus* sp.
Weeping juniper	*Juniperus flaccida*

Whitebrush	*Aloysia gratísima*
Wild rose	*Rosa* sp.
Wright's tickclover	*Desmodium psilophyllum*

Reptiles and Amphibians

Common Name	**Scientific Name**
Canyon tree frog	*Hyla arenicolo*a
Eastern black-necked garter snake	*Thamnophis cyrtopsis ocellatus*
Gray-banded kingsnake	*Lampropeltis alterna*
Mexican racer	*Coluber constrictor oaxaca*
Mottled rock rattlesnake	*Crotalus lepidus lepidus*
Northern black-tailed rattlesnake	*Crotalus molossus molossus*
Rio Grande leopard frog	*Rana berlandieri*
Spiny crevice lizard	*Sceloporus poinsetta*
Trans-Pecos copperhead	*Agkistrodon contortrix*

Butterflies

Common Name	**Scientific Name**
American lady	*Vanessa virginiensis*
Arizona sister	*Adelpha* sp.
JoBoni satyr	*Neominois carmen*
Mexican silverspot	*Dione moneta*
Mexican yellow	*Eurema mexicana*
Monarch	*Danaus plexippus*
Painted lady	*Vanessa cardui*
Pipevine swallowtail	*Battus philenor*
Sandia hairstreak	*Callophrys mcfarlandi* or *Sandia mcfarlandi*
Sleepy orange	*Eurema nicippe*
Variegated fritillary	*Euptoieta claudia*

Birds

Common Name	**Scientific Name**
Acorn woodpecker	*Melanerpes formicivorus*

American avocet	*Recurvirostra americana*
American kestrel	*Falco sparverius*
American robin	*Turdus migratorius*
American wigeon	*Anas americana*
Ash-throated flycatcher	*Myiarchus cinerascens*
Audubon's oriole	*Icterus graduacauda*
Band-tailed pigeon	*Patagioenas fasciata*
Barn owl	*Tyto alba*
Bell's vireo	*Vireo bellii*
Bewick's wren	*Thryomanes bewickii*
Black phoebe	*Sayornis nigricans*
Black-capped vireo	*Vireo atricapilla*
Black-chinned hummingbird	*Archilochus alexandri*
Black-crested titmouse	*Baeolophus atricristatus*
Black-crowned night heron	*Nycitcorax nycticorax*
Black-headed grosbeak	*Pheucticus melanocphalus*
Black-necked stilt	*Himantopus mexicanus*
Black-tailed gnatcatcher	*Polipptila melanura*
Black-throated sparrow	*Amphispiza bilineata*
Blue grosbeak	*Passerina caerulea*
Blue-throated hummingbird	*Lampornis clemenciae*
Blue-winged teal	*Anas discors*
Brewer's sparrow	*Spizella breweri*
Broad-tailed hummingbird	*Selasphorus platycercus*
Burrowing owl	*Athene cunicularia*
Bushtit	*Psaltriparus minimus*
Cactus wren	*Campylorhynchus brunneicapillus*
Canada goose	*Branta canadensis*
Canvasback	*Aythya valisineria*
Canyon towhee	*Pipilo fuscus*
Canyon wren	*Catherpes mexicanus*
Cassin's kingbird	*Tyrannus vociferans*

Cattle egret	*Bubulcus ibis*
Chipping sparrow	*Spizella passerine*
Cinnamon teal	*Anas cyanoptera*
Clay-colored sparrow	*Spizella pallida*
Common black hawk	*Buteogallus anthracinus*
Common goldeneye	*Bucephala albeola*
Common ground dove	*Columbia passerina*
Common poor-will	*Phalaenoptilus nuttallii*
Cooper's hawk	*Accipiter cooperii*
Crissal thrasher	*Toxostoma crissale*
Curve-billed thrasher	*Toxostoma curvirostre*
Dark-eyed junco	*Junco hyemalis*
Eastern screech owl	*Megascops asio*
Elf owl	*Micrathene whitneyi*
Flammulated owl	*Otus flammeolus*
Gadwall	*Anas strepera*
Gambel's quail	*Callipepla gambelii*
Golden eagle	*Aquila chrysaetos*
Gray vireo	*Vireo vicinior*
Great blue heron	*Ardea herodias*
Great egret	*Ardea alba*
Great horned owl	*Bubo virginianus*
Greater roadrunner	*Geococcyx californianus*
Green heron	*Butorides virescens*
Green-tailed towhee	*Pipilo chlorurus*
Green-winged teal	*Anas crecca*
Hepatic tanager	*Piranga flava*
Hooded oriole	*Icterus cucullatus*
Inca dove	*Columbia inca*
Indigo bunting	*Passerina cyanea*
Killdeer	*Charadrius vociferus*
Ladder-backed woodpecker	*Picoides scalaris*

Least sandpiper	*Calidris minutilla*
Lesser scaup	*Aythya affinis*
Lincoln's sparrow	*Melospiza lincolnii*
Loggerhead shrike	*Lanius ludovicianus*
Long-billed curlew	*Numenius americanus*
Long-billed dowitcher	*Limnodromus scolopaceus*
Lucifer hummingbird	*Calothorax lucifer*
Magnificent hummingbird	*Eugenes fulgens*
Mallard	*Anas playrhynchos*
Mexican jay	*Aphelocoma ultramarina*
Montezuma quail	*Cyrtonyx montezumae*
Mountain bluebird	*Sialia currucoides*
Mourning dove	*Zenaida macroura*
Northern cardinal	*Cardinalis cardinalis*
Northern flicker	*Colaptes auratus*
Northern goshawk	*Accipiter gentilis*
Northern mockingbird	*Mimus polyglottos*
Northern pintail	*Anas acuta*
Northern pygmy owl	*Glaucidium gnoma*
Northern saw-whet owl	*Aegolius acadicus*
Northern shoveler	*Anas clypeata*
Painted bunting	*Passerina ciris*
Painted redstart	*Myioborus pictus*
Peregrine falcon	*Falco peregrinus*
Phainopepla	*Phainopepla nitens*
Pied-billed grebe	*Podilymbus podiceps*
Pine siskin	*Carduelis tristis*
Pygmy nuthatch	*Sitta pygmaea*
Pyrrhuloxia	*Cardinalis sinuatus*
Redhead	*Aythya ameridcana*
Red-naped sapsucker	*Sphyrapicus nuchalis*
Red-tailed hawk	*Buteo jamaicensis*

Ring-billed gull	*Larus delawarensis*
Ring-necked duck	*Aythya collaris*
Rock wren	*Salpinctes obsoletus*
Ruby-crowned kinglet	*Regulus calendula*
Sandhill crane	*Grus canadensis*
Savannah sparrow	*Passerculus sandwichensis*
Say's phoebe	*Sayornis saya*
Scaled quail	*Callipepla squamata*
Scott's oriole	*Icterus parisorum*
Sharp-shinned hawk	*Accipiter striatus*
Slate-throated redstart	*Myioborus miniatus*
Snowy egret	*Egretta thula*
Solitary eagle	*Harpyhaliaetus solitarius*
Solitary sandpiper	*Tringa solitaria*
Song sparrow	*Melospiza melodi*
Sora	*Porzana carolina*
Spotted sandpiper	*Actitis macularius*
Spotted towhee	*Pipilo maculates*
Summer tanager	*Piranga rubra*
Swainson's hawk	*Buteo swainsoni*
Townsend's solitaire	*Myadestes townsendi*
Turkey vulture	*Cathartes aura*
Varied bunting	*Passerina veriscolor*
Verdin	*Auriparus flaviceps*
Vermilion flycatcher	*Pyrocephalus rubinus*
Vesper sparrow	*Pooecetes gramineus*
Violet green swallow	*Tachycineta thalassina*
Western bluebird	*Sialia mexicana*
Western kingbird	*Tyrannus verticalis*
Western meadowlark	*Sturnella neglecta*
Western screech owl	*Megascops kennicottii*
Western tanager	*Piranga ludoviciana*

Whip-poor-will	*Caprimulgus vociferous*
White-breasted nuthatch	*Sitta carolinensis*
White-crowned sparrow	*Zonotrichia leucophrys*
White-faced ibis	*Plegadis chichi*
White-throated swift	*Aeronautes saxatalis*
White-tipped dove	*Leototila vevreauxi*
White-winged dove	*Zenaida asiatica*
Wild turkey	*Meleagris gallopavo*
Wildson's phalarope	*Phalaropus tricolor*
Willet	*Catoprtophorus semipalmatus*
Williamson's sapsucker	*Sphyrapicus thyroideus*
Yellow-breasted chat	*Icteria virens*
Yellow-eyed junco	*Junco phaeonotus*
Yellow-rumped warbler	*Dendroica coronata*
Zone-tailed hawk	*Buteo albonotatus*

References

Baker, Rollin H. 1951. *Two New Moles (Genus Scalopus) from Mexico and Texas.* Vol. 5, No. 2 of *University of Kansas Publications, Museum of Natural History.* Lawrence, KS: University of Kansas.

——. 1956. *Mammals of Coahuila, Mexico.* Lawrence, KS: University of Kansas.

Brown, D. E., ed. 1982. *The Wolf in the Southwest.* Tucson, AZ: University of Arizona Press.

Burleson, B., and D. H. Riskind. 1986. *Backcountry Mexico: A Traveler's Guide and Phrase Book.* Austin, TX: University of Texas Press.

Culver, Melanie, Cora Varas, Patricia Moody Harveson, Bonnie McKinney, and Louis Harveson. 2009. "Connecting Wildlife Habitats across the United States–Mexico border." In *Conservation of Shared Environments: Learning from the United States and Mexico*, edited by Laura Lopez Hoffman, Emily D. McGovern, Robert G. Varady, and Karl W. Flessa, 83–89. Tucson, AZ: University of Arizona Press.

Delgadillo Villalobos, Jonás A., Bonnie Reynolds McKinney, Feliciano Heredia Pineda, and Santiago Gibert Isern. 2005. "Nest Record of *Sorex milleri* from Maderas del Carmen, Mexico." *Southwestern Naturalist* 50 (1): 94–95.

Gehlbach, Frederick R. 1981. *Mountain Islands and Desert Seas.* College Station, TX: Texas A&M University Press.

Gilmore, R. M. 1947. "Report on a Collection of Mammal Bones from Archeologic Cave-Sites in Coahuila, Mexico." *Journal of Mammalogy* 28: 147–65.

Goldman, Edward Alphonso. 1951. *Biological Investigations in Mex-*

ico. Smithsonian Miscellaneous Collections, vol. 115. Reprint. BiblioLife, LLC, Washington, DC.

Leopold, A. Starker. 1959. *Wildlife of Mexico: The Game Birds and Mammals*. Berkeley, CA: University of California Press.

Macdonald, Anita. 1981. *Mariposa: A Story of the Learmoths of Western Victoria and Mexico, 1834–1930*. Victoria, Australia: Colbert, Bain and Gaspar.

Marsh, Ernest G. Jr. 1936. "Biological Survey of the Santa Rosa and Del Carmen Mountains of Northern Coahuila, Mexico." Unpublished report to the National Park Service.

McCormack, J. E., G. Castañeda Guayasamin, B. Milá, and F. Heredia-Pineda. 2005. "Slate-Throated Redstarts (*Myioborus miniatus*) Breeding in the Maderas del Carmen, Coahuila, Mexico." *Southwestern Naturalist* 50: 501–3.

McKinney, Bonnie Reynolds, and Jonás A. Delgadillo Villalobos. 2005. *Manual para el manejo del oso negro mexicano: guía para manejadores*. Monterrey, Nuevo León, México: CEMEX.

McKinney, B. R., and J. A. Delgadillo Villalobos. 2007. "Preliminary Report on Maderas del Carmen Black Bear Study, Coahuila, Mexico." Western Black Bear Workshop 9, Raton, NM.

Mearns, Edgar Alexander. 1907. *Mammals of the Mexican Boundary of the United States*. Part I. Reprint. Bulletin 56. Washington, DC: Smithsonian Institution, United States National Museum.

Miller, Alden H. 1955. "The Avifauna of the Sierra del Carmen of Coahuila, Mexico." *The Condor* 57 (3): 154–78.

Onorato, D. P., and E .C. Hellgren. 2001. "Black Bear at the Border: The Recolonization of the Trans-Pecos." In *Large Mammal Restoration: Ecological and Sociological Challenges in the 21st Century*, edited by D. S. Maehr, R. F. Noss, and J. L. Larkin, 245–59. Washington, DC: Island Press.

Robbins, Michael. 2007. "The Treasure of the Sierra del Carmen." *National Wildlife* 45 (2): 30–33.

Taylor, Walter P., Walter McDougal, Clifford C. Presnall, and Karl P. Schmidt. 1946. "The Sierra del Carmen in Northern Coahuila, a Preliminary Ecological Survey." *Texas Geographic Magazine* 10 (1): 11–22.

Urban, E. K. 1959. *Birds from Coahuila, Mexico*. Lawrence, KS: University of Kansas.

Warren, Andrew D., George T. Austin, Jorge E. Llorente-Bousquets, Armando Luis Martinez, and Isabel Vargas-Fernandez. 2008. "A New Species of Neominois from Northeast Mexico (Lepidoptera: Nymphalidae: Satyrinae)." *Zootaxa* 1896: 31–44.

Wauer, Roland H. 1999. *Birder's Mexico*. College Station, TX: Texas A&M Press.

Index

Wayne, Robert, 17
Wild Sheep Foundation, 84–85
willet, 62, 105
Wolves of North America, 169
World War II, xx, 6

Yaqui Reserve, 75, 79–80
Young, Stanley, 169
yuccas at sunset, **P5**

Zacatecas, Mexico, 65
Zacatosa. *See* Tanque Zacatosa
Ziehe, Coy, 163
Zootaxa, 159